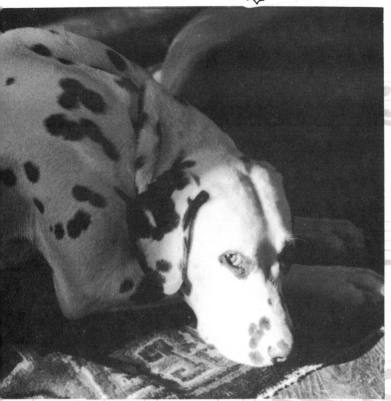

Dog Music

POETRY ABOUT DOGS

DOG MUSIC. Copyright © 1996 by Joseph Duemer and Jim Simmerman. All rights reserved. Printed in the United States of America. No part of this book may be used or reproduced in any manner whatsoever without written permission except in the case of brief quotations embodied in critical articles or reviews. For information, address St. Martin's Press, 175 Fifth Avenue, New York, N.Y. 10010.

Production Editor: David Stanford Burr

Design: Junie Lee

frontispiece photo *Zazen* by Roberto Diaz

Library of Congress Cataloging-in-Publication Data

Dog music : poetry about dogs / Joseph Duemer and Jim Simmerman, editors; photographs by Elliott Erwitt and other photographers.
     p.   cm.
    ISBN 0-312-15113-6
     1. Dogs—Poetry.   2. Human-animal relationships—
Poetry.   3. American poetry.   I. Duemer, Joseph.
II. Simmerman, Jim.   III. Erwitt, Elliott.
PS595.D63D56   1995
811.008'036—dc20   95-41060
                                             CIP

First St. Martin's Griffin Edition: February 1997

10 9 8 7 6 5 4 3 2 1

The editors of Dog Music are donating fifty percent of their profits from royalties to animal welfare organizations that care for dogs. Additionally, many of the poets in this volume generously waived reprint fees so as to permit the editors to donate the entirety of those fees—more than $2,000—to such organizations.

Books by Joseph Duemer

The Light of Common Day (Windhover)
Customs (Georgia)
Static (Owl Creek Press)

Books by Jim Simmerman

Home (Dragon Gate)
Once Out of Nature (Galileo)
Moon Go Away, I Don't Love You No More (Miami University)

EDITED BY JOSEPH DUEMER
AND JIM SIMMERMAN

ST. MARTIN'S GRIFFIN ☙ NEW YORK

CONTENTS

OLD BLUE *Anonymous*

Had an old dog and his name was Blue.
Betcha five dollars he's a good'n too.

Here Blue, you good dog you.

Showed him the gun and I tooted my horn,
Gone to find a possum in the new-ground
    corn.
Old Blue barked and I went to see,
Cornered a possum up in a tree.

Come on Blue, you good dog you.

Old Blue died and he died so hard,
Shook the ground in my backyard.
Dug him a grave with a silver spade,
Lowered him down with a golden chain.
Every link I did call his name.

Here Blue, you good dog you.
Here Blue, I'm coming there too.

"Several years ago in a hotel bar in Denver . . ." Such an opening sentence might sound like the beginning of a mystery novel, perhaps with a western setting. But when completed ". . . two poets sat talking about their dogs." you will begin to understand the genesis of this anthology. In fact, it wasn't very far into the first round of Anchor Steam that the two poets were making a mental list of their favorite poems about dogs. What could be more natural? It has turned out to be a pretty long list, as this fat puppy of an anthology testifies. Even before those bottles of Anchor Steam in Denver, though, I had been thinking of making a collection of dog poems. In fact, the impulse may have come over me upon seeing Jim's "Fetch" in *Poetry* in 1985. Early on, I had already identified Gerald Stern's "The Dog," John Updike's "Dog's Death," Richard Wilbur's "The Pardon," and Greg Kuzma's "The Return," along with several other wonderful poems. That informal list of poems in my head, combined with Jim's enthusiasm and the mental list he'd been compiling, led eventually to this book.

Compiling an anthology, like living with dogs, will teach you patience. When we had collected a fairly fat batch of dog poems, I began writing to literary agents. Most agents, of course, do not bother with poetry because there is no money in it, but I assembled a list of twelve or so likely candidates and sent a sample of the manuscript off to them. Most of the responses were quick—and negative. One agent wrote, with uncanny literary judgment, "When I first read your letter I at first thought this might make a fun trade book of verse about dogs, but after reading the poems I discovered this is real poetry. . . ." She was, she said, sorry she couldn't consider publishing such a book. Real poetry indeed. Fortunately, a few days later a letter arrived from Sydelle Kramer on the letterhead of Frances Goldin, literary agent. Sydelle thought *Dog Music* contained real poetry, too; but she also thought the book should be published. Jim and I are grateful to Sydelle for her enthusiasm, and especially for her patient guidance, for this has been a long process for all concerned.

It is astonishing how many good dog poems there are. As Jim says, almost every poet has written one. Initially, our job was easy, we just grabbed everything we could find. And though we solicited work from only a few poets, word got out. There was a period during which dog poems arrived in the mail nearly every day. We have not been able to include everything we might have wished. Many good poems arrived after we had had to call a halt—we have a file of thirty or forty more poems that might have gone into this book if we had the space. To all the poets who sent us work we haven't been able to include, our thanks. There is a platonic universe in which the ideal version of *Dog Music* has existence, and your poems, there, are included.

Each of the poets represented here has learned something from a dog, and these poems are the records of that encounter. It is surprising how many such encounters result in moral insight. Stephen Dunn, in his poem "Some Things I Wanted to Say to You," writes "Did you know / that a good dog in your house / can make you more thoughtful, / even more moral?" I won't speculate on this philosophical issue, except to note that even without such a sense, encounters with dogs seem to evoke such insights in humans—or at least in poets. In his poem "Consciousness," Czeslaw Milosz has written,

> Our humanness becomes more marked then,
> The common one, pulsating, slavering, hairy. . . .

Dogs, perhaps because we have brought them halfway over toward the human, can sometimes take us halfway back to the urgencies of the animal body, the urges of the animal mind. It can only do us good. One note, however: This book will break your heart, for it is full of elegies for innocent beings who moved among us. Luckily, several canines also take comic turns among these pages.

The poems here are all by Americans, with exception of a few that have achieved a presence in the language through translation; all are from the twentieth century. While poets, regardless of culture or historical moment have probably always noticed dogs, it does seem that recent American poets have adopted the dog as a kind of heraldic metaphor for certain virtues. That's what the evidence of these poems suggests to me, at any rate. Virtue and vice—moral qualities—are inescapable when we encounter dogs, with whom we have such a long and ambiguous history.

I didn't grow up around dogs. Oh, there were my uncle Joe's coonhounds in a pen, wild and noisy. And I suppose there were one or two dogs who hung around for a while, then ran off. I never formed any attachments to dogs when I was young. I was, the truth be told, a little bit afraid of them. Perhaps that helps explain the passion with which I embrace all things canine now in middle age.

It was not until 1985 that I made my first close dog acquaintance, and then it was because my wife Carole announced one morning that she thought we needed a dog. Carole *had* grown up with a succession of dogs—from basset hound to Saint Bernard—and our newly established household felt empty to her without one, I think, though to say such a thing is not her way. That afternoon we went to the county shelter in San Diego and took home with us a three-month-old Australian shepherd/terrier mix, gray and white. She knew him when she saw him. He was due to be "put down" the next day, we were told. The only evidence his previous owners left behind was his name, Mingo, which we preserved, thinking it would be a presumption to change it, and the phrase "could not keep" on the card in the shelter office.

He was—and is—a rambunctious dog. As soon as we got him in the car he tore up a map and a magazine, and later he would tear up a few other things, including two sets of curtains. He was delighted, though, to be out of his cage, away from the smell of death. Mingo has taught me a number of things over the years, but chief among them is delight. My work on this anthology, then, is dedicated to Mingo. In addition to Mingo, Maude, and, more recently, the Weezer have helped keep me warm on cold winter nights and have contributed their canine joy to our household.

Among the humans who deserve credit for this project, I want to thank my wife, Carole Mathey, for typing parts of the manuscript, as well as for putting up with my chronic procrastination and resultant anxiety; Stacy Pappano performed further wordprocessing chores, for which I thank her. My coeditor Jim Simmerman has been a boon companion throughout the process of putting this book together. Sydelle Kramer has already been mentioned, but it is not too much to say, *this never would have happened without her.* To Judy Arajs, companion to more dogs and other lucky animals than I can count, once my landlord, now my friend, my gratitude—her spirit informs this entire project.

—JOSEPH DUEMER

SUCH GOOD COMPANY

Joe will have told the story of how this book came to be: a sort of two-man anthology version of the *Our Gang* episode in which the "gang" finds stored in a barn an array of vintage clothes and costuming, and in which one kid suddenly blurts—like a comic strip light bulb going on over a head—"Hey, kids, I've got an idea; let's put on a show!" What follows is the show. And I feel lucky as any kid with a few props and a little imagination to be involved in its production.

Lucky or blessed. For it seems to me a kind of blessing to be permitted to pursue one's passions; and I've always been passionate for dogs—dogs have been a constant in my family and my life for as far back as I can remember. But I'm passionate too for poetry—that other, if slightly less long-standing, constant in my life. Dogs and poetry, both, have afforded me an abundance of companionship and solace down the years. Both have made me ache—sometimes with grief, most often with joy. And so, in being permitted to merge these two passions here, I feel—to quote the Bard—twice blessed; I feel like one lucky dog.

Among the pleasures of collecting these poems over the past several years has been to discover that almost everyone has a dog poem, and that almost all of them are good! What follows in this kennel of verse is a wide assortment of recent works in English—by poets ranging from the famous to the obscure—which may or may not be *about* dogs, but which consistently *use* dogs as central figures of metaphor and for meditation. Thus, the tones of these poems are considerably varied, running from the elegiac to the contemplative to the comic. Thus, the true "subjects" of these poems include love, art, family, politics, religion. . . . Whether or not you are a dog fancier, I think you will find herein poems that are varied, moving, intellectually stimulating, and aesthetically pleasing; poems that admirably represent the vitality and scope of modern and contemporary verse. Though if you *do* like dogs—even, perhaps, if you have not heretofore been a fancier of poetry—this collection should come as a real treat.

I would like to acknowledge here a number of people who assisted in the process of seeing *Dog Music* into print. First and foremost, I wish to thank my coeditor and collaborator Joe Duemer—who shared the vision—for all his hard work and good spirit. I also wish to thank Paul Janeczko, Bill Matthews, Ed Ochester, and Chase Twichell for their sage advice regarding the business of anthology-making. Thanks too to Alison Deming and

Eric Pankey, who kindly provided valuable information necessary to secure permissions for some of these poems. And thanks to Keith Cunningham, folklorist, for contributing the sources of and texts to a number of versions of "Old Blue." To Sydelle Kramer and Frances Goldin Literary Agency, and to Bob Weil and St. Martin's, my thanks for believing in this project. Perhaps most of all, I wish to thank our contributors, who of course wrote the poems in the first place, but who were also generous, enthusiastic, and helpful above and beyond the call.

Lastly, I wish to dedicate this book to my family, from whom I learned to cherish the company of dogs, and to that honor roll of stouthearts— Penny, Jolly I, Jolly II, Mona, Lo, Maddy, and the Bandit—that kept me such good company all these years.

—JIM SIMMERMAN

Dog Music

THE DOG AT THE CENTER OF THE UNIVERSE

PAMELA ALEXANDER

Husky-masked, bologna-tongued, Pfoxer
settles her bulk on the bed and props
a long jaw on the window sill
like the muzzle of a pioneer's rifle,
heavy to hold alone; pivots it
as she examines the gestures
of grass and birds. The universe,
itself created expressly for her perusal,

is putting the finishing touches
on an August dusk.
Red light slides up
shafts of grass, hesitates, then
springs: the luminous tips blink dark.
The field cools and ticks like an engine
just turned off. She scans it
not for Indians but for rabbits,
those fascinating creatures
with ears so like her own—long, soft,
alert. Surely rabbits and she have interests
in common, issues to discuss with little fear
of disagreement! But the difficult cousins
have so far fled her well-meant attention
and all invitations to play.

She sighs. She closes her eyes and allows
her weight on this side of the fulcrum
to swing her face toward the moon
—rabbit-light, muse to whom she sometimes
raises voice as well as nose.
I would not care to wager
that she does not register some delicate

moon-scent
in that moist, oversized chemical analyzer
that is the furthermost point of both
her physical construction
and her sensory appreciation
of the above-mentioned universe.

Her paws work in a dream. She shoots
after rabbits, or moons.

Muzzle-loader, she slams
her own dinner home; lifts
that magnificent sniffer
to consider my choice of spices
for the soup; longs to get my dinner
in her sights, too.

CONSOLATION

PAMELA ALEXANDER

in the voice of John James Audubon, 1832

The violence in Civilized parts is worrisome. We have old
New York Papers describing riots, I advise
thy absence from that country. We are well away,
our last named place being St. Augustine
a poor sandy town profuse of oranges, some buildings
entirely in a plaster made of course ground shell.
The shadows of orange trees against brilliant walls
were pleasing, though the fruit sour.
The weather is unruly, unreasonably hot
one day & cold the next. In consolation I have seen
a new Eagle I hope to kill tomorrow.
                              What dangers we have
are predictable, from Nature who can be used
against herself. I do not walk into water
unless it be a living bouillabaisse. Though my legs
are bruised where fish slap in panic
there presence ensures no alligators. Plato suffers,
for when hot his habit is to plunge into the nearest water
& swim slowly, looking sleepy, for hours,
& I prevent him. I bind his paws with leather
because they are raw, cut by the shells of raccoon oysters,
common here; he has been bit in the face twice
by Ducks, one he dropped and I shot again.
We are all Abraded, Lehmann & Ward & I, from shells
& sand & insects which are hugely plentiful
& we are welts & salt-sore scratches everyone. Please send
more good Wollen socks, the marsh & mud
& tide flats we travel wear them urgently.

THE DOG

JOHN ALLMAN

We could hear him out there past the lilacs,
all day dying beneath the Douglas fir.
His long, hound-and-mongrel body almost
flat, breath rattling in his lungs like broken
machinery, how did he manage getting
up, limping to his dish, eyes like banked fires?
Next day, the cat leaped at a low-flying
wild canary, caught that song in her jaws,
while he met us in the garage, his throat
flaccid, ears drooping, his pinched look of shame,
his fault, such slow death not ours to forgive.
We said nothing at dinner, mentioned no
creatures lost to us, cats with twisted
nylon strings strangling the small intestine,
the white mouse buried in a parking lot,
the pheasant that flew into our screen door,
through it, and broke her neck. We thought we had
plenty of room for voiceless departures.
Each night now in dreams we hear his old man's
cough; run to the blazing pines where no sun
brings fire to sleep; feel the harsh light
leave our bones, as we enter the dark
caves of his eyes, the tunnel of his howl.

RUNNING

JOHN ALLMAN

Up into mist before dawn, panting on the dark
road, inhaling the odors of sleep and empty
barns, the cling of hay and manure, body and breath
opening, shouldering forth, pressed into the swell

of light, my jointed luminous stripes like the bones
Halloween children wriggle at one's door, faces
masked with horror: I take the curve, brush the frosted
chrysanthemums, a cold finger probing my knee,

cords tightening in calf and ankle, I'm entering
fog, this milky air, sudden cataracts filling
my eyes, darkness dissolved from trees, I rush between
white columns, footfall echoing as if I ran

on all fours, the woods closing around me as I
race the sun, my spirit loose inside a blue skin.

A Dog after Love

Yehuda Amichai

After you left me
I let a dog smell at
My chest and my belly. It will fill its nose
And set out to find you.

I hope it will tear the
Testicles of your lover and bite off his penis
Or at least
Will bring me your stockings between his teeth.

Ye Bruthers Dogg

Jon Anderson

Hodain D. Dogg
& Toolie Orlen

Ye dogg, O'Toole,
Who hath not work
At love nor arte
Nor goeth schule
Sayeth with fart
At Gulden Rulle,
"Be it bitch or bisquit
Or platter stewe,
Ye palate alone shal guide yu."

Ye dogg, Hodain,
Forgoeth bone
Nor doth distain
To moanne,
". . . for winde & raen,
Ye snow & fogg,
Ye seasons, sunn,
& world roll on,
But ye dayes a' dogg be not longe,"

Bruthers Tew,
Ye slimm Hodain,
& fatte O'Toole,
Beneath fense
Diggeth hole.
Into ye world
Ye Bruthers danse;
Nor wuld return
Ye fatte O'Toole & slimm Hodain.

Sune is report
Brothers Tew

Doth run amok
I' neighborhude.
Cautions O'Toole,
"Hodain, ye may barke,
May scowle & be rude,
But do not bitte
Ye hand what giveth dogg fude."

Tho all complane
A' Bruthers Tew,
No winde nor raen
Doth drive them homme.
Then sayeth Hodain
To Bruther, "O'Toole,
Tho we hath been frende
Thru thik & thinn,
Dogg needeth sume love from Mann."

So ende ye song
A' Bruthers Tew.
Away they had flown
& back they flewe.
Reclineth i' yard
Thru seasons & sunn,
Thru winde & raen,
Ye snow, ye fogg,
O'Toole, Hodain, ye Bruthers Dogg.

Dog Song

Anonymous (Pima Indian)

version by Joseph Duemer after a translation by Frank Russell

Our songs begin at nightfall
when the wind blows from the south—
the wind is strong,
bending my tail toward the north.

Butterfly wings begin to fall.
Butterfly wings are falling
that hurt me when they fall
& my suffering is greater than . . .

See the little dogs come running!
See the poor dogs come running!
See the horsemen coming after,
see the horsemen come laughing!

THE DOGS

SONDRA AUDIN ARMER

Fence in the dogs—
They shed, they steal,
They cannot be
Brought in to heel.

Fence in the dogs—
They drool, they beg,
They claim the land
With lifted leg.

Fence in the dogs—
They prowl and sniff.
Their greedy ways
Will lead to grief.

Fence in the dogs—
They growl and snap.
Glove your hand,
Raise your whip.

Fence in the dogs—
They bare their teeth
And fight each other
To the death.

Fence in the dogs,
For when unleashed,
The dogs pursue
Their human lusts.

THE LAST NIGHT YOU ARE GONE

RENEE ASHLEY

The dogs
are wild
with loneliness.
From the hallway
where the light
burned out
four days ago, the bed
looks so long
and unpeopled
as Interstate 80,
at Rawlins,
the time
we came
East
and were
stranded
in the storm.

I sleep
on the couch
the last night
you are gone
as if sleeping
with the dogs
in an unaccustomed
place without you
would bring
us close,
but each car
that goes by,
invisible
in the dark,

makes the dogs go
crazy and they leap
to greet you
all night
long; no one
sleeps. My job
is to tell them,
over and over, you
are not coming.

By tomorrow
we'll braid ourselves
together, leg
thrown to hip,
arm to the crown
of the head,
a lazy knot
of comfortable
indifferent body
and be glad.
The dogs will lie
in dark masses
on the dark floor;
they'll see you
back, know
nothing changed
for good. They
only knew
you were
missing, knew
you were gone.
In their sadness,
they howled
like black
shadows of dogs
against a too bright
moon.

LOST DOGS

RENEE ASHLEY

Sweetheart,
    The fog is pudding-thick and the lost
dog, the black one we coaxed home from the park, is wild with
    unhappiness
(no one calls him sweetheart). He hoisted his withered leg
and pissed circles like smoke rings on the sofa; he was howling,
    I swear, "I'll be Home
for Christmas." Some sort of miserable miracle. But that's how
    it is here.
Anyway, we've got to stop stealing lost dogs. It makes them
    melancholy

and, besides, the house is getting smaller all the time.
    Melancholy
seems the rule now. How long have you been gone? The lost
dog, the gray one, has come home; I'd figured he was dead but here
he sits, riddled with bootjack, steamy with wanderlust. He may
    just know
by heart, now, the scent of comfort, these mild fires that burn
    at home.
Remember your last departure? Remember the final leg

of your already too-long journey? The blind hound who'd lost his
    leg
to the snowplow had left us all cold and melancholic—
the bad news hit you hard. The dog healed; but you were home-
sick to begin with and, back then, anguish was the face we wore
    for everything we lost.
But the dog still hobbles the rock ledge; sightless, three-
    legged, he doesn't know
he's a candidate for sorrow. There's a tricky lesson here:

something about grace or humor, something about the here-
and-now. About patience. You see, it's all in the
      understanding: legs
it would seem, aren't the issue. No,
I think it's the absence, and how, because we're only human, we give
      in to melancholy.
It's about how loneliness and sorrow set the soul loose
      to seek what it just can't seem to find at home.

Well, we just keep waiting for some word, hoping these notes find
      you heading home-
ward. I tell you about the strange dog with the ragged ear
      who, obviously, was lost
and hungry, not hurt, but tired, worn out from his wandering? By
      the time he got here his legs
were shaky and the pads of his feet were raw. For two days he
      slept; he seemed sort of melancholy
when he woke but, then, suddenly, he up and ran off with the
      grizzled pup from down below. No

one's seen them for a week now. The man who kept the grizzled
      one doesn't seem to know
he's gone. I keep driving around the lake, but the dogs aren't
      there; perhaps they've found a home.
I'm trying not to think about it. I worry about the ones who go,
      and I get melancholy.
It's the fog, I think that makes me so sad. It's difficult to
      see clearly here.
Between the mist and the low stone fences, we're lucky we don't
      break a leg
just taking the short hike to the main road for mail. We've lost

the knack of the smooth stroll. No, we're too aware that here
and there trouble hangs thick as this homegrown fog—and we
      don't need a leg-
up on blindness or melancholy. No, Sweetheart, we stay home to
      keep from getting lost.

DOG'S TALE

JEFF AVANTS

How well must I
have prepared for this tale
that'll likely be judged,
not by content,
but by how well it's groomed.

Once, it was not a tale
but destiny barking out
of an open hole
on a hospital table.

And all the world was
warm and sterile, honest,
and uncritical as a bone.

But somewhere, somehow, I learned
to speak,
to roll over.
I became a regular stand-up
guy!

All that's past. Now,
every dog has its due.
And I admit, it makes me
shake, a little,
but I too must bear
my tale;
submit.

I submit to you,
it's late,

incomplete,
but will you accept, dear reader,
what my dog didn't eat?

George by Valerie Shaff

SUNBATHING

DAVID BAKER

from Sonnets from One State West

My neighbor's new store-bought dog yaps again,
hungry, crazy with heat, maybe both,
stretching his short chain until he chokes.
The little dab of sunshine I lay down in
has drifted away, into the shrubs,
but I'm not budging. *I'm surely dying!*
my cruel neighbor's pup keeps yelping

and, so help me, I suppose he is,
his poor dog's life ticking away like my own.
I guess I'll stay right here in the cool shade
and let him cry for us both—our sad,
single bodies, our chains and our bones,
all burning down to ash and grime
quickly enough on their own sweet time.

Phantom Dog

Angela Ball

A woman heard something being torn,
came out shouting "Get away!"
Saw a ripped garbage bag, a bone, a dog
skittering backwards: shy thing,
tall and pure gray, a double strand of teats
following the belly's scroll,
elegant as a violin's. This in the instant
before the dog ran, hips veering
as if the ground shuddered under them.
"Here, Girl, here! Get your bone."

In dogless quiet, a breeze
lavished the branches, the trees fluent
with green, even in January.

GIACOMETTI'S DOG

ROBIN BECKER

She moves so gracefully on her bronze legs
that they form the letter *M* beneath her.
There is nothing more beautiful than the effort
in her outstretched neck, the simplicity of the head;
but she will never curl again in the comfortable basket,
she will never be duped by the fireplace and the fire.

Though she has sniffed out cocaine in the Newark Airport,
we can never trust her good nose again.
She'll kill a chicken in her master's yard,
she'll corner a lamb in the back pasture.
She's resigning her post with the Seeing Eye.

Giacometti's *Dog* will not ask for water
though she's been tied to a rope in Naples
for three days under the hot sun.
Giacometti's *Dog* will not see a vet
though someone kicks her and her liver fills with blood.
Though she's fed meat laced with strychnine.
Though her mouth fills with porcupine quills.

Giacometti's *Dog* is coming back
as a jackal, snapping at the wheels
of your bicycle, following behind in her
you-can't-touch-me-now-suit.
Giacometti's *Dog* has already forgotten
when she lost the use of her back legs
and cried at the top of the stairs
and you took pity on her.

She's taking a modern-day attitude.
She knows it's a shoot-or-get-shot situation.

She's not your doggie-in-the-window.
She's not racing into a burning house or taking your shirt
between her teeth and swimming to the beach.
She's looking out for Number One,
she's doing the dog paddle and making it
to shore in this dog-eat-dog world.

KILTY SUE

MARCK L. BEGGS

Instincts jammed by lack of sheep
in this region, she attends to babies, ducklings—
anything small and in need of care.
A border collie whose eyes, opposite
shades of brown, offer the look
of a slightly retarded devil-dog. And,
if you must know, she bites people:
my brother, presumably, because he was mean
to me at a younger age; the UPS man
because he carries a package too quickly towards
my pregnant sister; my mother-in-law, I suppose,
to keep in shape. And various relatives
and strangers—Kilty Sue reminds them
of the precise location of their Achilles tendon.
Mind you, she never actually rips it out,
but merely offers a sharp touch. Like a pin-prick
only deeper, her bites spring out
from a sudden vortex of silence. When Kilty Sue howls—
in a voice high and piercing as a drunken soprano,
and you wish your ears would just drop off and die—
you are safe. She is protecting you.

THE BOOK OF THE DEAD MAN
(#68)

MARVIN BELL

1. ABOUT THE DEAD MAN'S DOG

The dead man, *that* man, consorted with canines in the turmoil of a
   derangement sensed by few others.
The mongrel was apt, the mutt, the half-breed is best, the hybrid, the
   mixture—being those of an underclass to which the dead man
   belongs.
The dead man's dog is immediate, primary, without tedious human
   calculation.
The dead man's dog follows his nose, his tongue lags but accompanies,
   his owner's voice mixes with the sighing of the browning leaves.
The dead man's dog is housebroken, barnbroken, fieldbroken,
   lawnbroken but is free to go.
The dead man's dog keeps a tight leash on his master, dragging him to
   every clandestine murmur, every rumor of affection.
The dead man's dog has the wherewithall to violate those senseless codes
   meant to make a man or woman stay.
To the contrary, the dead man's dog shakes hands, he fetches, he heels,
   also he behaves and misbehaves in human proportions.
The dead man's dog plays dead.

2. MORE ABOUT THE DEAD MAN'S DOG

When there is no more approbation, no license, no all-time immunity,
   no obedience or disregard, no loyalty that is not also the pick
   of the litter, no luck but dumb luck then okay it's not a show, and
   spunk is what it takes.
It takes the dead man an eternity to romp, meanwhile he learns a mutt's
   moxie.
Oh pretty dogs that reap the rage of benefactors in good times.
Oh dogs shorn of the outdoors, oh clipped, oh shaggy shaggy shaggy.
The dead man's dog does not sit up and beg.
The dead man's dog is the hybrid of now and later, bred to be good
   with children, eager, vigilant.

Hound and buddy, enthusiast of dishes and scraps, perch for fleas,
    station of sanity, trained to disobey in the nick of time—the
    dead man's dog runs beyond reason.
His is the virtue of the undersides of logs.
He readies his bones for the passage to the underworld.
He rolls before the fireplace, the whole house his sarcophagus, his face
    lit like that of an Egyptian jackal.
The dead man's dog's teeth are nine-tenths of the law.
His claws are the quills whose marks will be the stuff of history.
His tail is a brush for which the wide day is his canvas.
Eagerly, the dead man lies down with dogs, observer of puppy love and
    dog song.
The dead man's dog is a little bit of alright, a wagging yes, a cause of
    whistling and waving, cupped hands and come-when-called.
He bestirs the dead man's fortitude.

WHEREVER YOU ARE

MARVIN BELL

1.

A thin silver whistle
and the dog can hear it, but it's late
for Prince and the puppy that got loose.
Prince had a bed behind the store
and a friend at the butcher. Got himself
hit by a car in the stomach
and came within a gloved hand of the end
but faced up to the chloroform
with a dogged friendliness that signaled health
and sapped him for another week.
He was my father's, and knew things.
The way a dog's ears will stand up,—
that's the way Prince caught on and stood up.

2.

He had this thought and that thought,
I'm sure of it. Another dog was a summer
many years later, and I could ask him
to find my son in the woods. Dogs who saved
whole families in fires, who walked home
for hundreds of miles, who died within
a week or two of their owners—
they could hear the place where their absence
reshaped the air, that grave sound.

I have heard a few things before
they were said. It's nothing like the giraffe,
who says nothing, or the dolphin, who hears
it all: it's an open ear
ready for the slightest squeeze of air:
a cough of vocal muscles tensing,

a rubbing in the throat, the muscular.
It's the mutt in me, that's all.

To be "man's best friend" might be
to listen so well it needn't be said.
To hear up high, to know the thing that isn't

yet. Then what must it mean
to be death's best friend . . . ?

WALKING WITH VIRGIL

DAVID BIESPIEL

The joints in rigor mortis, lips sliced back,
Teeth-rows like hardened salt, toes spread, stiff fur
Cloaked with an oily-like gray and still flat,
The eyes wide-open as it dropped
From his long, dog mouth at my Wellington.
This mouse in limbo long before Virgil
Found it in the ivy patch, on the path
Below the woods. It was death he smelled,
Its circle of thin-boned living long gone,
And the day nearly lost over the brink.
Virgil looked up and wagged once: a gift,
I thought. Food for the cave, for the pack.
The mouse kept silent on the ground, staring.
Virgil looked down, looked back, then snatched it
Again and trotted down the brook
Where the dusk was soaking in shadelessly
And dropped it in the water. It sank.
Small, circular ripples rose in its place.
As if to keep it in mind forever,
Virgil stared, retriever's head tilted, tail
Still—a dog's memory is not so good.
And the light flecking back behind the trees
Made seeing too impure, and the darkness
Coming on enclosed us with its heavy arc.
The circles of the earth had found their places.
So when he came back to me, came back
From that other world, it was as if to say
His stray days were over. Then up the path,
Wagging his tail at half-mast and trotting.
And I, so as not to go astray, following.

PINK DOG

ELIZABETH BISHOP

Rio de Janeiro

The sun is blazing and the sky is blue.
Umbrellas clothe the beach in every hue.
Naked, you trot across the avenue.

Oh, never have I seen a dog so bare!
Naked and pink, without a single hair ...
Startled, the passersby draw back and stare.

Of course they're mortally afraid of rabies.
You are not mad; you have a case of scabies
but look intelligent. Where are your babies?

(A nursing mother, by those hanging teats.)
In what slum have you hidden them, poor bitch,
while you go begging, living by your wits?

Didn't you know? It's been in all the papers,
to solve this problem, how they deal with beggars?
They take and throw them in the tidal rivers.

Yes, idiots, paralytics, parasites
go bobbing in the ebbing sewage, nights
out in the suburbs, where there are no lights.

If they do this to anyone who begs,
drugged, drunk, or sober, with or without legs,
what would they do to sick, four-leggèd dogs?

In the cafés and on the sidewalk corners
the joke is going round that all the beggars
who can afford them now wear life preservers.

In your condition you would not be able
even to float, much less to dog-paddle.
Now look, the practical, the sensible

solution is to wear a *fantasía*.*
Tonight you simply can't afford to be an
eyesore. But no one will ever see a

dog in *máscara* this time of year.
Ash Wednesday'll come but Carnival is here.
What sambas can you dance? What will you wear?

They say that Carnival's degenerating
—radios, Americans, or something,
have ruined it completely. They're just talking.

Carnival is always wonderful!
A depilated dog would not look well.
Dress up! Dress up and dance at Carnival!

Carnival costume.

LOSSES

CATHY SMITH BOWERS

Each morning, as sun calls back
from the grass its lent vapors,
that crew of little spirits rising for work,
my retriever begins his ritual of cheeps and chirps
like a nest of sparrows or those biddies
parents buy at Easter for their children
knowing they will die. He won't soil his pen,
so by the time I've had my coffee
and staggered to the yard to let him out,
he is desperate, bolts through the gate
and across the path he has worn in our lawn.
He circles and circles, sniffing out
the perfect spot, lifts his leg, then lopes,
as he was trained, into the woods,
to the sweet mulchy floor of pine and cedar.
Again he sniffs, circles, then curves
his tail-end under like a giant hook or comma.
The Muslim in him faces east
where the scarab sun climbs the sky's moist web.

It doesn't seem right, watching him.
Hunched like an aborted fetus. Straining.
His legs trembling. His soft eyes
averted from my insensitive gaze. The way one summer
in Indonesia, that woman, bathing
beneath the ashy rise of Gunung Agung,
turned shyly away as our cameras continued to click.
She had waded, naked, with her youngest to the bank
where she stooped like a little frog, emptying
his bowels onto the sand. Was it then I knew
I would never have children? Could not bear

at so close a range those leaks
and solvents. Would get instead a dog
I could train to go off into the woods
carrying deep into shadow the body's chronic losses.

The Lost Dogs of Phnom Penh

Kay Boyle

Do not stab my heart like this, scabby vagrants, garbage hounds, waiting
For the truck to sail on its tide of odor into port.
At one-thirty in the morning (now, as then), truck wheels are hushed
    by the monsoon rains
Or the clamor of the Asian stars, and you are there. You have
No growl in throat, no snarl on lip, you do not shout names at one
    another,
Death, the ineluctable, being so near. You wait on brittle haunches,
    dream
Of the fine enamel of eggshells not quite scraped of their contents; of
A strip of lettuce glistening with the solid gold of oil.

Back in the land of packaged meats, at one-thirty in the morning (now,
    as then),
I think of you, of your ribs curved like the wicker of crickets' cages,
The desiccated crickets of your hearts no longer chirping behind the
    bars.
I think of you, lost dogs, of the eternal wishbones of your breasts.
Under the streetlights you form a motley alphabet,
Unsuitable for use in any language. When one of you lies down,
He draws the wooden links of a tail around his elbows.
His body shapes a weary "m," humped like a camel, in defeat.
Another of you becomes the letter "u," like a sick lamb curved across
    the shepherd's
Forearm. But nowhere among you can I find a "t," high as a whistle
    keening
Beyond the reach of human ear; nowhere among you is there an "e,"
The beginning of that ironic "enough." I seek these letters
To complete the brief word "mute" that is closed, fleshless,
Bloodless, in the cold anvils of your jaws. At one-thirty in the morning,
The radio in my kitchen tells me that America, my country, is the
    garbage capital of the world.

Lost dogs of Phnom Penh, cry out, cry out, as men cry out
Across the intricate frontier of broken, still unbroken Vietnam,
Under the same unfaltering stars!

THE SUBSIDY

WILLIAM BRONK

Well, I don't know: that crazy dog,
puppy-boy inexpressibly
overjoyed—many mornings I wake
like that, loving the light, the new day.

I know not to. Suppose I had the power,
what would I do? It isn't that things are wrong
—though they are—but that there isn't a way,
any conceivable way, to set them right.

The hopelessness. Anything's defeat
is always its own terms which seem they should win
as often they do. How else should we see their defeat?

These are the only terms we think of,
hopeless terms. Our life, such as it is,
is elsewhere. Welcome morning. Give me joy.

DOGFIGHT

CHARLES BUKOWSKI

he's a runt
he snarls and scratches
chases cars
groans in his sleep
and has a perfect star above each eyebrow

we hear it outside:
he's ripping the shit out of something out there
5 times his
size

it's the professor's dog from across the street
that educated expensive bluebook dog
o, we're all in trouble

I pull them apart
and we run inside with the runt
bolt the door
flick out the lights
and see them crossing the street
immaculate and concerned

it looks like 7 or 8 people
coming to get their
dog

that big bag of jelly with hair
he ought to know better than to cross
the railroad tracks.

THE DOGS ON THE CLIFFS

MICHAEL BURKARD

They are there
after having long departed
from their memory, and whether there is any memory
of a master is hard to say, for they were
born into an island
which was poor, could not support the birth of dogs
except with the whiteness of the tourists'
faces, a whiteness like the wallets
and purses, the loose change of the lives
which brought them and their own memories to this island,
summer after summer,
injury after jury.

The jury on the island says this:
the dogs may roam each summer
til it is obvious they are a menace,
chickens attacked, an occasional tourist
attacked, lingering now in small
pathetic packs. And thus they are herded
to the sea from the cliffs above,
enticed perhaps by some ice memory
(surely the local islanders don't entice them fully
with a little meat, are they that hungry?)

—an ice memory of the dogs of the year before,
and the fall before that, in the month of September,
upon an island which despises animals anyway—

and the dogs are brought to the cliffs and herded off.
To the sea. To the rocks and sea below.
It is a long drop, even for a dog.

I did not so much live upon this island
as hear this story, more vividly told, with a particular
dog which followed a particular man—the dog even did a double
take one summer—when the man reappeared on Ios after departing
for a month to Athens—and the dog followed the double take—
just seeing the face twice—with following.

So this story is not mine, but I feared a man would never tell it—
though versions of stories like this must abound.

I can hear the stories on the cliffs,
I can hear the lamps wailing sometime
much later in the winter, in winter
when the animals are dead, all of them, all
the past times down below
near the rocks off Ios.

Now the ice memory wakes: the jury reports
in a different dream
that the town and villas are sold out
already for still another summer,
another history for history,
another past
for past.

Today, after only
glancing
at the morning paper

I thought of the phrase
history repeating itself,

thought if history repeats itself
it is still the same history,
more repetition, no
history

because it's the same history
the same hysteria
which could include even me
again.

A GUARDIAN TANYA

THOMAS CARPER

Guardian animals . . . adorn tombs
in every civilzation, accompanying the soul
on its crossing of the river of death.
KENNETH CLARK, Animals and Men

Sensing when I must travel, she refuses
To sleep downstairs. She comes into the bedroom,
Nuzzles her biscuit into a corner,
Circles twice, and lies down at my feet.
Her sleep is sound, and I sleep soundly too,
As if we two were sculptures in an abbey,
Memorialized by a forgotten artist
Who understood necessities of friendship.
It's likely she will die before I die,
And though I have no faith in streets of gold,
I have half-confidence that I will meet her
On this side of a bridge across death's river,
Letting arriving spirits pat and scratch her,
Or stretching out, her head between her paws
As if for sleep, but with her eyes wide open,
Watching, waiting, sure that I will get there,
Sure that I will find her among thousands,
Coming gladly with a leash to link us
So we can go to death as on a walk.

JOGGING WITH TANYA

THOMAS CARPER

There are disadvantages, for Tanya
Is curious about other things than I am—
Smells in bushes, rubbish, other dogs
Barking as though she threatened to attack them,
And evidence that horses came before us.
Nevertheless, we run mostly together;
When I pull on her leash, she usually
Will leave whatever stopped her, uncomplaining.
My interests are more cosmical than hers are:
I ponder human suffering on the inclines,
The universe's beauty on the downgrades,
The way life is an uphill-downhill matter,
And how it can be told of in iambics.
I like to think I am the more amused,
And that my speculations will be valued
By gods whose work of health I am assisting
With my exertions, though they are exhausting,
And though when we turn finally at our driveway
We are both glad to walk, and I am sweating.

HAIKU

HAYDEN CARRUTH

Reversions, always
reversions. When wet, dogs smell
fishy, wives doggy.

UNDERGROUND THE DARKNESS IS THE LIGHT

HAYDEN CARRUTH

When I first started out to make what later became known as Hayden's
    Runaway Pond, I borrowed
Baldy Langdell's little Cat that he used mostly for sap-gathering in his
    hillside sugar orchard
Over in Waterville, but he had a blade on it, and once I got the hose
    connections tight
It worked well. I had a good spot, and Pop Foster, the county agricultural
    agent,
Agreed. "Ideal," he said. It was a gentle downslope sort of folded in
    the middle, where a brook
Ran straight down from a spring in the woods behind, a good spring,
    never known
To run less than nine quarts a minute in the driest season. I went to
    work.
"Now watch you don't scrape too deep in the hardpan," Pop said, and
    I nodded.
I pushed dirt to all sides, but mostly to the front, where the embankment
    would be highest,
Like a dam. Pop showed me how to set up the standpipe with a wing
    valve at the bottom, the outlet pipe
Headed straight forward under the bank and into the brookbed again.
    It didn't take long,
A day and a half with the dozer. Then I set the valve just a mite open
So some of the water would continue flowing out into the brook and
    on downstream,
But enough would catch in the pond to fill it. I watched. Slow, very
    slow, only a puddle
After the first two days. But I expected that. I sowed the banks to rye,
    clover, and orchard grass.
Of course that summer, after the pond filled and water spilled into the
    standpipe so I could close the bottom valve,

It was a sterile pond. But the next spring I had frogs, big ones and little
 ones, and that summer
What I call the purple water flower seeded in and some bulrushes on
 the far side. Then the following spring
The stoneflies hatched, and the mosquitoes, so I stocked some minnows
 and brim. By the end of July
I had a muskrat hole on the upper back just over the water-line. Next
 spring I stocked brookies,
A couple of dozen, and they took to it, and I used to go at twilight
 with my part-shepherd bitch Locky
To feed those trout bits of hamburger. How they rose to it! Locky would
 stand downbank
With her front paws extended and bark at them, and sometimes I
 thought maybe the trout
Were barking back. It was a fine pond, alive, a going concern. Swallows
 from Marshall's barn
Skimming the surface. Once I saw a heron. Then two summers later I
 saw the water
Was sinking. "Must have scratched the bottom a mite hard," Pop said.
 It went down slowly
The same way it had filled, but after six weeks it was all gone, nothing
 left
But mud and the brook trickling across the bottom and down into a
 hole I could see plain enough,
Jagged, about eight inches across. No fish, no grogs. They must have
 gone down too.
Down into the earth, a live pond flowing into all those channels and
 chambers down there.
Strange to think of. Locky went trotting and sniffing here and there on
 the sun-dried mud,
Looking half scared. "Don't that beat all?" Marshall said. And I said,
 "Yes, it does."

YOUR DOG DIES

RAYMOND CARVER

it gets run over by a van.
you find it by the side of the road
and bury it.
you feel bad about it.
you feel bad personally,
but you feel bad for your daughter
because it was her pet,
and she loved it so.
she used to croon to it
and let it sleep in her bed.
you write a poem about it.
you call it a poem for your daughter,
about the dog getting run over by a van
and how you looked after it,
took it out into the woods
and buried it deep, deep,
and that poem turns out so good
you're almost glad the little dog
was run over, or else you'd never
have written that good poem.
then you sit down to write
a poem about writing a poem
about the death of that dog,
but while you're writing you
hear a woman scream
your name, your first name,
both syllables,
and your heart stops,
after a minute, you continue writing,
she screams again.
you wonder how long this can go on.

BECAUSE THE DOG DEMANDS

SIV CEDERING

I leave the lamplit lane and walk into the dark.
I cannot detect the scent of pheasant, fox,
the doe who lost her way
or the creature that screeched the copulating cry
that woke me in the night,
but he pulls me on past subtleties as refined,
perhaps, as Botticelli or Boccherini
to a canine mind.

When I turn to go back, he does his dance
in the tall grass and squats on trembling legs,
as vulnerable to the world—and intent on doing—
as any human being.
At the end of the leash, I tilt my head
looking up. Only a bit of information
separates the stars in their patterns
from the fireflies that float in the dark, mating.

The woman you went to see
and the man I carried
like a stone in my gut
are almost forgotten.
Through tangles of bittersweet,
I see the light from our porch
and the windows lit up,
waiting.

DOG DAYS

SIV CEDERING

The farmers in Vermont
reach for guns in their sleep.

Mrs. Ketchum woke, one morning,
to a hundred dead sheep.

Which dog had gnawed
each gnawed-off face?

    Sirius
    is rising.

If a dog sleeps on your pillow
you will dream his dream.

My husband tosses in his sleep
sleeping on my pillow.

Which act that I have forgotten
is he living in his dream?

The dog is waiting by feet.
It is hot. I am counting sheep.

AFTER MY LAST PAYCHECK FROM THE FACTORY, TWO THIN COUPONS, FOUR TIN DOLLARS, I INVITED OLD LIU FOR AN AFTERNOON MEAL.

MARILYN CHIN

for the Chinese Cultural Revolution
and all that was wrong with my life

I ordered vegetables and he ordered dog,
the cheapest kind, mushu, but without the cakes.
I watched him smack his greasy lips
and thought of home, my lover's gentle kisses—
his faint aroma, still with me now.

I confided with a grief too real,
"This is not what I expected"
and bit my lip to keep from crying,
"I've seen enough, I want to go home."
But suddenly, I was seized by a vision

reminding me why I had come: two girls
in uniform, red bandannas and armbands
shouting slogans and Maoish songs,
"the East is red, the sun is rising;"
promises of freedom and a better world.

Trailing them was their mascot of Youth,
a creature out of Doctor Seuss or Lewis Carroll,
purplish pink, variegated and prancing.
I stood in awe of its godlike beauty
until the realist Liu disrupted my mirage.

"It's the dog I ordered and am eating still!"
he mumbled with a mouthful of wine.
And as it came closer I saw the truth:
its spots were not of breeding or exotic import,
but rampant colonies of scabies and fleas,

which, especially red in its forbidden country,
blazed a trail through the back of its woods;
and then, its forehead bled with worms,
so many and complex, as if *they* did its thinking.
I rubbed my eyes, readjusted the world . . .

Then focused back on his gruesome dish
trimmed with parsley and rinds of orange.
One piece of bone, unidentified which,
stared at me like a goat's pleading eye
or the shiny new dollar I'd just lost.

Old Liu laughed and slapped my back,
"You American Chinese are hard to please."
Then, stuck his filthy chopsticks into my sauce.
"Mmmm, seasoning from Peijing, the best
since opium," then, pointed to a man

sitting behind me, a stout provincial governor
who didn't have to pay after eating the finest
Chinese pug, twenty-five yuan a leg.
He picked his teeth with a splintered shin,
burped and farted, flaunting his wealth.

Old Liu said with wine breath to kill,
"My cousin, don't be disillusioned,
his pride will be molested, his dignity violated,
and he as dead as the four-legged he ate
two short kilometers before home."

HOMAGE TO OUR LADY OF THE STRAYS

DAVID CITINO

*How terribly wrong some love
can go,* she must have thought
that last week, hold up
in the kichen, hoarding
in the vault-cold oven
one last chunk of Velveeta
and heels of Wonder Bread.
Even her dreams began growling.

Fifty years she'd given
to strays, every crumb to squirrels,
lice-ridden dove and pigeon
dingy as pitted statues,
house finch and jay stained
gunmetal gray. She gave names:
Wayne Newton, Jackie O and *Cher,
Ron* and *Nancy* and *The Duke.*

Through two good hardwood inches
they gnawed their way to her,
devoured even teeth and hair
in their famine, long bones
of arm and thigh all her remains.
The mailman began to wonder,
junk mail throttling the box,
Congratulations, Lucky Winner!

Come in to claim your prize.
The pound, in a matter
of hours, put to sleep all 34.
Anthropophagic, News at Eleven claimed.
Shelties, poodles, pit bulls, mutts:

their souls rose from the chimney
to embitter rains downwind.
The house can't be cleaned.

The Board of Health put it
on its list of histories to be razed,
if arsonists or derelicts
don't get there first
and offer this address to flames.
I pray they do, for what
could be a more fitting end
to so metropolitan a rite?

O My Lady, there's no poverty
like yours, no excuse for cities.
I don't even know where they've put
your bones, clean as ivory
in the well-endowed museum
beside the dark lovely park
of druggies and crazed rapists.
Have mercy on us, patron saint of age,

of old ones made to live and die alone.

IF JOAN OF ARC HAD A DOG

ROBIN CLARK

would she have heard, would she
have noticed Michael's fiery presence
amid the beans, cabbages, and onions,
between the straight rows
of her father's garden, his body
shining just beyond her shoulder—

would she have known
what name to choose, whispering it
as she entwined her fingers
within the dog's hair, thick and wooly,
reminding her of the watching sheep—
you who refused to be vowed to any man,
would you have loved this animal
as no other—would you have
forgotten the marks your father struck
upon you, his accusations and curses
and your mother's betrayal—
would you have bothered to leave Domrémy
to seek your sword at Fierbois—
you were a fearless woman.

would you have chased each other
through the wildflowers, cascading
down along the Meuse, barely touching,
becoming conveniently lost
to come home safe, late enough—
or would you have stayed in the fields,
listening for the words between the ringings
of the church bells, hoping the dog
would not bark at the wrong time—

DOG LIGHT

WILLIAM CLIPMAN

Ignored, like the green flash of the fly.
Passes across a dog's eyes, a beacon
to warn our thought-bound brains away
from the unthinking rock. Blinks on
like the porch light
for a short visit from intelligence.
Skull-glow animates the mask adjusted by
a tilt of the head: a moon ray
through shifting clouds, a consequence.

Burns pale white—
what wolves know each other by.
And stays, sometimes, to mock our dumb surprise,
belie such false obedience.
White teeth, bone light, dog's eyes.

DOG

BILLY COLLINS

I can hear him out in the kitchen,
his lapping the night's only music,
head bowed over the waterbowl
like an illustration in a book for boys.

He enters the room with such etiquette,
licking my bare ankle as if he understood
the Braille of the skin.

Then he makes three circles around himself,
flattening his ancient memory of tall grass
before dropping his weight with a sigh on the floor.

This is the spot where he will spend the night,
his ears listening for the syllable of his name,
his tongue hidden in his long mouth
like a strange naked hermit in a cave.

RCA VICTOR

BILLY COLLINS

The dog is seated by the Victrola
listening, head cocked

to the voice of his master
and thinking

how different he looks today
smaller, like a box
and his head an ornate
megaphone.

Where are the legs
he needs to walk me
where are the hands
that throw my ball

the dog wonders
trembling slightly.

IN THE 9TH YEAR OF THE LITERARY WAR

HENRI COULETTE

to Charles

Well, poetry lovers of America,
this is about Heinz
and my stepping on his tail.

He was dreaming
57 variations
on that theme eternal,
the theme of Heinz,

and I was drunk,
having trouble with my feet,
having had trouble
with my head . . .

Lowell and Ginsberg and Bly were dead,
Justice was missing,
so I turned to Wright,

whose face loomed
in the light
the dead gave off . . .

and it happened!
I mean, it really happened.
(Poetry lovers,
would I lie to you, would I?)

The Pekingese next door took up the cry,
and the Afghan down the block,
and the Bull beyond,
and the cry went forth.

Dog to coyote to wolf,
the cry went forth,
Able to Baker to you.

Tulle by Valerie Shaff

NIGHT THOUGHTS

HENRI COULETTE

in memory of David Kubal

Your kind of night, David, your kind of night.
The dog would eye you as you closed your book;
Such a long chapter, such a time it took.
The great leaps! The high cries! The leash like a line drive!
The two of you would rove the perfumed street,
Pillar to post, and terribly alive.

Your kind of night, nothing more, nothing less;
A single lighted window, the shade drawn,
Your shadow enormous on the silver lawn,
The busy mockingbird, his rapturous fit,
The cricket keeping time, the loneliness
Of the man in the moon—and the man under it.

The word *elsewhere* was always on your lips,
A password to some secret, inner place
Where Wisdome smiled in Beautie's looking-glass
And Pleasure was at home to dearest Honour.
(The dog-eared pages mourn your fingertips,
And vehicle whispers, *Yet once more*, to tenor.)

Now you are elsewhere, *elsewhere* comes to this,
The thoughtless body, like a windblown rose,
Is gathered up and ushered toward repose.
To have to know this is our true condition,
The Horn of Nothing, the classical abyss,
The only cry a cry of recognition.

The priest wore purple; now the night does too.
A dog barks, and another, and another.

There are a hundred words for the word *brother*.
We use them when we love, when we are sick,
And in our dreams when we are somehow you.
What are we if not wholly catholic?

THE WORD

MARK COX

I get in between the covers as quietly as I can.
Her hand is on my pillow and I put my face as close
as I can without waking her up. We made salad yesterday
and her fingertips still smell of green pepper and onions.
I feel homey, almost safe, breathing this, remembering
the way we washed the vegetables under cold water, peeled,
then sliced them with the harmless little knife her sister
gave us for Christmas. I feel childish and gently pull
the blanket over my head, barely touching my lips
to the short, ragged fingernails she chews while talking
to her mother on the phone. These days there's so much bad news
from home. Old people who keep living and living awfully,
babies who stop breathing for no reason at all.
I am so close to her that if I were to speak one word
silently, she would feel it and toss the covers to one side,
and for this reason I'll say nothing as long as I can.
Let the sheet stiffen above us, I have nothing to say.
Not about their lives or my own life.
Not about the branches so weighted with snow
they don't brush our window anymore.
Not about the fact that the only way I can touch anymore
at all, the only way I can speak, is by trying not to.
"what's left, what's left, what's left," my dog breathes
in his sleep. Lately I snore badly in a language
only he understands. I've been trying so hard to teach,
I've been trying so hard to switch bodies
with the young people in my classes that last week, when the dog
woke me and wanted to go out, I took his face in my hands
and told him not to be afraid. "You know so much already," I said.
"You are talented and young, you have something to give people,
I wouldn't lie to you."
Rita told this story as we sat around the salad with friends,

repeating again and again how the dog closed his eyes and basked.
Sleep is also the only place I can type with more than three
fingers, I said. But I thought, it's true, all this,
I speak best and most fully in my sleep. When my heart
is not wrapped in layer after layer of daylight, not prepared
like some fighter's taped fist.
She sleeps, her hand next to my mouth, the number
for the 24-hour bank machine fading on its palm.
The word starts briefly from between my lips, then turns back.
The word sifts deeper into what my life is.

HISTORY

MARK COX

Solitude is a cold pear I eat
in the dark, knowing
that were my dog here,
he would wake near the bed
and wait patiently for me
to remove the stem
and hand down the core.

I might hear him licking there,
for an hour or more.
The taste forgotten, then remembered,
in the grain of the floor.

CRYING WOLF

MARY CROW

Something seems to be moving
through the flock, speck across
the false snow on the hill's crest,
bleating faint and pathetic,
as Laddie and I head for the flock.

Why do we go for our own throats?
I woke with my head aching,
haranguing myself, hating myself.
Now I walk through thin air:
Real problems, I say, wolves, death—

this morning's heifer stuck belly-deep in mud
icy cold from mountain runoff,
even her bellow shivering,
as she cried to me. I pulled her out
with the tractor, too late;

her temperature could not be raised.
When I catch my own cry in my head,
is that my animal self?
Last week when I bent over a sick calf,
he was hot, damp, a little lump
on the straw in his stall.

Will he die? I gave him a shot,
tried to get him to eat, tried to shut
out that voice, its claim to misery.
Misery, I told it, of your own making!
Well, back to the sheep, Laddie

running ahead, happy I would say

from a human perspective.
A wagging tail anyway, a body
that gambols and stops, jumps
and runs, looks back for me.

And my voice inside—what
happened to it? As we moved
away from the house, and I followed
Laddie's joy, a field
filled me inside, huge and white,
no wolf anywhere in sight.

DOG MUSIC

ROBERT DANA

Was it worth it, I ask myself—
all those years of making music
for the deaf? All those somber
and brilliant colors worked
onto canvases for the blind?
Maybe I was composing in a key
only dogs could hear, or cats.
Colors for the multifaceted
eyes of spiders, ants, or flies.
Maybe it was art for saints.
So what if fame is ash; summer
smoke. How much do you need?

A DOG SLEEPING ON MY FEET

JAMES DICKEY

Being in his resting place,
I do not even tense
The muscles of a leg
Or I would seem to be changing.
Instead, I turn the page
Of the notebook, carefully not

Remembering what I have written,
For now, with my feet beneath him
Dying like embers,
The poem is beginning to move
Up through my pine-prickling legs
Out of the night wood,

Taking hold of the pen by my fingers.
Before me the fox floats lightly,
On fire with his holy scent.
All, all are running.
Marvelous is the pursuit,
Like a drizzle of nails through the ankles,

Like a twisting shout through the trees
Sent after the flying fox
Through the holes of logs, over streams
Stock-still with the pressure of moonlight.
My killed legs,
My legs of a dead thing, follow,

Quick as pins, through the forest,
And all rushes on into the dark
And ends on the brightness of paper.
When my hand, which speaks in a daze

The hypnotized language of beasts,
Shall falter, and fail

Back into the human tongue,
And the dog gets up and goes out
To wander the dawning yard,
I shall crawl to my human bed
And lie there smiling at sunrise,
With the scent of the fox

Burning my brain like an incense,
Floating out of the night wood,
Coming home to my wife and my sons
From the dream of an animal,
Assembling the self I must wake to,
Sleeping to grow back my legs.

DOG UNDER FALSE PRETENSES

WILLIAM DICKEY

Not very affectionate; she likes to kiss,
but not to stay still long and be petted.
Yet if she is shut outside, she barks angrily.
If I move from one room to another, she moves too.
Is it a confusion in her history?

Now, after these months, I have her papers
from her first owner. Why was she given up?
The pet groomer who had her, and the birds, and Norman
the Great Dane, od'd on speed, disappeared,
was found later in a mental hospital.

It has worked out in different ways.
Norman is in the High Sierra, killing his own deer.
The birds have been killed by a raccoon, who slit
their nylon cage, ate most of them. Imogene,
like a mafia *capo*, is taking over.

Nothing is as it was guaranteed to be.
She is not a Lhasa Apso, she is a Shih Tzu.
She has grandfathers and great-grandfathers, she has
her own number with the American Kennel Club.
She is in fact known, an aristocrat.

For the first three days I thought she was
timorous, elderly, a quiet dog
who would sit by the fireplace of evenings, who
could be taught to knit. After all these years
I should recognize, when I see it, shock.

I could and do recognize resilience.
Out of the wound of loss, of nobody,

it takes little to make her again feel
a person, to bark angrily, to say
"I am a person again. Let me in."

What were those weeks like, in the almost
unattended pet shop, where there was food
but nothing else? Svidrigailov says of eternity
"What if it were only a small bathhouse
full of spiders?"

It is something, at least, to be in time
rather than eternity. We may howl,
child, dog, at being bathed, tied up
while we dry. Yet it is a touch.
Why bark if you know there is no one listening?

So the aristocrats must have
crossed the Russian border to Shanghai,
knowing that they were nothing they had been before,
must have got jobs as *maîtres-d'hôtel*,
as café waitresses.

Must have come out of shock, into
a knowledge, tentative at first, that
it was possible to be human, must have said
to the world that was not their world "I have revised
my conceptions of being human. Let me in."

For many, there will have been those weeks
in the abandoned pet shop, when one was neither
owned nor believed in. There will have been
a break in the continuity of life.
"I was myself, or nothing. Nothing, then."

And as the Jews walked in their ritual order
to the chambers that would displace them, a space
opened in the middle of life, empty. Then
to one woman boarding the train, a neighbor
finally offered a sandwich.

A raccoon has eaten the birds, we do not
all survive, there is final and less than final.
Imogene will survive, she is fortunate.
I have given her a name other than her own name.
It is a device to change her luck.

And perhaps there is no place in her memory
to remember when she was nothing. If so, good.
She has now a plastic beetle that squeeks to play with.
She plays with it enthusiastically, wants other people
to play with her. It may be enough.

HOPE

WILLIAM DICKEY

At the foot of the stairs
my black dog sits;
in his body,
out of his wits.

On the other side
of the shut front door
there's a female dog
he's nervous for.

She's the whole size
of his mind—immense.
Hope ruling him
past sense.

HOW TO LIKE IT

STEPHEN DOBYNS

These are the first days of fall. The wind
at evening smells of roads still to be traveled,
while the sound of leaves blowing across the lawns
is like an unsettled feeling in the blood,
the desire to get in a car and just keep driving.
A man and a dog descent their front steps.
The dog says, Let's go downtown and get crazy drunk.
Let's tip over all the trash cans we can find.
This is how dogs deal with the prospect of change.
But in his sense of the season, the man is struck
by the oppressiveness of his past, how his memories
which were shifting and fluid have grown more solid
until it seems he can see remembered faces
caught up among the dark places in the trees.
The dog says, Let's pick up some girls and just
rip off their clothes. Let's dig holes everywhere.
Above his house, the man notices whisps of cloud
crossing the face of the moon. Like in a movie,
he says to himself, a movie about a person
leaving on a journey. He looks down the street
to the hills outside of town and finds the cut
where the road heads north. He thinks of driving
on that road and the dusty smell of the car
heater, which hasn't been used since last winter.
The dog says, Let's go down to the diner and sniff
people's legs. Let's stuff ourselves on burgers.
In the man's mind, the road is empty and dark.
Pine trees press down to the edge of the shoulder,
where the eyes of animals, fixed in his headlights,
shine like small cautions against the night.
Sometimes a passing truck makes his whole car shake.
The dog says, Let's go to sleep. Let's lie down

by the fire and put our tails over our noses.
But the man wants to drive all night, crossing
one state line after another, and never stop
until the sun creeps into his rearview mirror.
Then he'll pull over and rest awhile before
starting again, and at dusk he'll crest a hill
and there, filling a valley, will be the lights
of a city entirely new to him.
But the dog says, Let's just go back inside.
Let's not do anything tonight. So they
walk back up the sidewalk to the front steps.
How is it possible to want so many things
and still want nothing? The man wants to sleep
and wants to hit his head again and again
against a wall. Why is it all so difficult?
But the dog says, Let's go make a sandwich.
Let's make the tallest sandwich anyone's ever seen.
And that's what they do and that's where the man's
wife finds him, staring into the refrigerator
as if into the place where the answers are kept—
the ones telling why you get up in the morning
and how it is possible to sleep at night,
answers to what comes next and how to like it.

Two Dogs

Stephen Dowdall

One procelain white,
One gold.
Just introduced, they
Circle each other
Sniffing.

It was a long ride
From Ohio to these mountains.
"You look good."
"You look Good."
"Good to see you."
"Good to see You."

Two dogs take turns
At dominance
And submission.
"I'll let you chew
At my throat,
If I can chew at yours."

Your soap, your towel,
I'm just another reckless boarder.
Listen, I hear from the bathroom,
"You're prospecting illegally,
On land not your own."

Two dogs
Follow the fence.
One pisses on a post.
The other covers it.
Scent stakes territory,
Where you piss is home.

Listen,
I soiled your towels,
Turned your soap to
Suds in a shell-shaped dish.
Last night, drunk on your whiskey,
I held your razor to my throat.
Here's Mine.

DOGS AT DOG BEACH

JOSEPH DUEMER

1.
My dog has found some other dogs to romp
with, one a muscled, bow-legged dalmatian,
the other, several sorts of spaniel leaping
in one mottled body. From where I stand

the waves are distant, tide out but moving
up the reach of gray-brown sand slicked
with light that's almost oily, sun a hot
pink smudge on the horizon. What makes

this a scene? This is where the slow river
comes down, after its confinement between
dikes through the environs of the city, to
the sea. Estuaries are always mysteries.

2.
A dog never swims twice through the same
afternoon. Surge after surge of ocean
pushes up river, and I am wet to my knees
with all the evidence I need that Earth

spins in an establishment of certain forces
that separate the firmament from shifting sand.
Out along the surf line the three dogs cut
a long arc, breakneck, then plunge into

the noise of hissing foam, breasting the waves
that, petered out, wash against my legs
where I stand, a little in the river, swirls
of backwash flattening into dusk around me.

3.
It turns out the Dalmatian is stone deaf.
Its owners, a young couple with a baby,
tell me it is cued to things it cannot hear
by following the spaniel's eyes. The girl strips

to a bathing suit and walks into the river;
lying back into the movement of the tide,
she backstrokes toward the bigger breakers
uncoiling silently out there. As she swims,

she calls the dogs, thrashing the water, and
they come bounding, all three, raising silver
plumes with their forelegs, concerned, or just
going along to please themselves, and us.

4.
The dogs emerge, tails dripping, and shake,
starting with their tails, themselves. They trot
along the bank as the girl rises from the water
and moves toward us, dragging her hands lightly

across the inky surface. She's still fat
from pregnancy, and the mystery of this
image—slashed pink wakes of light trailing
from her fingers—cannot be taken lightly.

Dogs are this world's great innocents, they understand
not irony, are color-blind; at dusk the ocean silvers
into shades of gray—we start home together,
trotting through the features of a simple universe.

SOMETHING LIKE HAPPINESS

STEPHEN DUNN

Last night Joan Sutherland was nuancing
the stratosphere on my fine-tuned tape deck,
and there was my dog Buster with a flea rash,
his head in his privates. Even for Buster
this was something like happiness. Elsewhere
I knew what people were doing to other people,
the terrible hurts, the pleasures of hurting.
I repudiated Zen because it doesn't provide
for forgiveness, repudiated my friend X
who had gotten "in touch with his feelings,"
which were spiteful and aggressive. *Repudiate*
felt good in my mouth, like someone's else's tongue
during the sweet combat of love.
I said out loud, *I Repudiate*, adding words
like *sincerity, correctness, common sense.*
I remembered how tired I'd grown of mountaintops
and their thin, unheavenly air,
had grown tired, really, of how I spoke of them,
the exaggerated glamour, the false equation between
ascent and importance. I looked at the vase
and its one red flower, then the table
which Zennists would say existed
in its *thisness*, and realized how wrong it was
to reject appearances. How much more difficult
to accept them! I repudiated myself, citing my name.
The phone rang. It was my overly-serious friend
from Syracuse saying *Foucault, Foucault,*
like some lost prayer of the tenured.
Advocates of revolution, I agreed with him, poor,
screwed for years, angry—who can begrudge them
weapons and victory? But people like us,
Joan Sutherland on our tapes and enough fine time

to enjoy her, I said, let's be careful
how we link thought and action,
careful about deaths we won't experience.
I repudiated him and Foucault, told him
that if Descartes were alive and wildly in love
he himself would repudiate his famous dictum.
I felt something like happiness when he hung up,
and Buster put his head on my lap,
and without admiration, I was sure, stared at me.
I would not repudiate Buster, not even his fleas.
How could I? Once a day, the flea travels
to the eye of the dog for a sip of water.
Imagine! The journey, the delicacy of the arrival.

THE DOG'S MUSIC

RUSSELL EDSON

The rich hire orchestras, and have the musicians climb into trees to sit in the branches among the leaves, playing Happy Birthday to their dogs.

When the manservants come with birthday cakes, they are told not now, do not dare disturb me when I am listening to my dog's music.

I was just wondering, sir, if I should light the candles.

I said not now. Do you want to distract me from my dog's music? Don't you realize that this is his birthday, and that it's been a whole year since his last birthday?

Shall I just put the cake in his feeding bowl, sir?

You are still distracting me from my dog's music. I wonder why you do it. This is not your birthday. Why are you trying to attract my attention?

But, sir, the cake . . .

But do you think I want my dog to see me talking to you while his music is being played? How would it seem to you if I talked to the dog while your music was being played?

So sorry, sir. I'll take the cake back to the house . . .

Oh no, it's gone too far for that—Sic' em, sic' em cry the rich to their dogs.

And so the dogs of the rich leap on the serving men, who cry, help, to the rich, who reply, not now, not now, the dog's birthday is passing into history, with all its marvelous music!

THE DOG

A dog hangs in a kitchen, his back stuck to the ceiling. An old woman tries to work him loose with the handle of her broom.

The dog struggles, but the more he struggles the deeper he sinks into the ceiling. He growls and snaps. He implores and whines, swallowing and chewing; his tongue curling in and out of his mouth, as though he lapped water . . .

Finally only the dark little dots of his footpads can be seen. They hear him whining inside the ceiling . . .

The dog . . . ? says the old woman.
The dog is ruined says her husband.
The dog . . . ? says the old woman.
It's the ceiling, says her husband.
The dog . . . ? says the old woman.
It ate the dog, the ceiling ate the dog, says her husband.
The dog . . . ? says the old woman.
. . . The dog, says the old man.

AFTERNOON WALK

RON EZZIE

"There are snakes everywhere," she says
pointing at two small coins of water
down an embankment.

We step over soggy mulch and
green spines pointing up,
a few twisted open into
skunk cabbage.

"I can't get too close," she says,
blues eyes wide,
blonde hair spread
in a breeze,
afraid one might slide
down her boot,
probe its serpent head
against her heel.

"Okay, let's go," I say,
black mud sucks
at our soles as
we turn,
head back for the top where
the gravel and tar road
crumbled from too much winter and neglect
makes bikers walk
as far as the trailer
where the logger from Ontario
raises huskies
for sledding.

And there

halfway up
where every marsh marigold and
leafless branch could be seen,
we find them,
scattered in the brush,
unwanted lives tossed
from some car,
tiny ears flapped down so still,

4 puppies,
                    black
      brown
            tan and
                            white,
strangely peaceful,
pink bellies
warming in the sun,
a little futher down
a shepard mix
lies on its side with
a dark red hole above
her brown ear,

guilty of fertility,
the thaw and
moistening of spring
which sent so many tongues
to lick and taste
the flow
of ground water
which rose in her.

I kneel,
whisper, "Why?"
expecting her tail will wag
and prove miracles
happen here
where more trees than houses
crowd my mind.

DOG

LAWRENCE FERLINGHETTI

The dog trots freely in the street
and sees reality
and the things he sees
are bigger than himself
and the things he sees
are his reality
Drunks in doorways
Moons on trees
The dog trots freely thru the streets
and the things he sees
are smaller than himself
Fish on newsprint
Ants in holes
Chickens in Chinatown windows
their heads a block away
The dog trots freely in the street
and the things he smells
smell something like himself
The dog trots freely in the streets
past puddles and babies
cats and cigars
poolrooms and policemen
He doesn't hate cops
He merely has no use for them
and he goes past them
and past the dead cows hung up whole
in front of the San Francisco Meat Market
He would rather eat a tender cow
than a tough policeman
though either might do
And he goes past the Romeo Ravioli Factory
and past Coit's Tower

but he's not afraid of Congressman Doyle
although what he hears is very discouraging
very depressing
very absurd
to a sad young dog like himself
to a serious dog like himself
But he has his own free world to live in
His own fleas to eat
He will not be muzzled
Congressman Doyle is just another
fire hydrant
to him
The dog trots freely in the street
and has his own dog's life to live
and to think about
and to reflect upon
touching and tasting and testing everything
investigating everything
without benefit of perjury
a real realist
with a real tale to tell
and a real tail to tell it with
a real live
        barking
                democratic dog
engaging in real
              free enterprise
with something to say
              about ontology
something to say
          about reality
                  and how to see it
                      and how to hear it
with his head cocked sideways
              at streetcorners
as if he is just about to have
              his picture taken
                  for Victor Records
          listening for

His Master's Voice
and looking
like a living questionmark
into the
great gramaphone
of puzzling existence
with its wondrous hollow horn
which always seems
just about to spout forth
some Victorious answer
to everything

HOUND SONG

DONALD FINKEL

Three nights in a row
he fed on our leavings
rattling our cans
till we let him in

wherever we went, he went
to the end of his rope

we let him in
we let him out
we let him in again

one night at the corner, he paused
the old bones squared
his ears cocked soft to hear
what it said, it said
nothing I could hear

in the streetlight his life
hung loose on his bones
a hammock of shadow

we let him out
we let him in
we let him out again

The New Dog: Variations on a Text by Jules Laforgue

Carol Frost

I.
The new dog's sugary breath warms my neck,
milkflecks on his muzzle.
Day begins, lighting his lavender eyes.
Relaxed as a child, he seems to look
out across the yard at the sun's ascent.

The hour of last dreams when the bare elm
is tinged with gold. With this dog Max
I look out across the yard. I think
of newborn everywhere.
I think of Max who will wander
with curiously human eyes in the roses;
then imagine myself coming out of the garden,
going in place of Max to the road
and walking under a car.

I imagine entering this grave:
the full weight of Max counterpoised against
the glance he turned away.

II.
You shovel the graveyard dirt too far
as if it were obscene to dig
a hole for Max, who is lying there
beside the rose bower, his ribs
and heart unstirred, his eyes
wide-open, tinged by sunrise.

The hour of reverie when the elm
is lit with gold. The day begins.

Think of Max in another realm
too remote for touch, wandering in
a garden. Think of his dark eyeball
surveying the darkness for us all.

Now the grave must be
refilled with the full weight of Max.
Beyond the sky's blue filigree
you cannot see the zodiac
when with sunlight in the air
you cover up his final stare.

KISSES

RICHARD FROST

When Edna, our cleaning lady, arrives, she kisses
our golden retriever full on the mouth, holding
his head in her hands and rubbing her lips
back and forth against his, maybe even
French kissing him. She moves back a half inch
and murmurs, in a voice so amorous that though
she is very ugly, probably even too ugly for the dog,
it raises the hairs on the back of my neck,
and the dog braces his legs and looks
sideways and up at me. "My baby," she croons.
"My baby, how have you been this week?
I have some scraps for you." What interests me most
is that the dog, Zachary, is clearly embarrassed.
When she lets go to reach into her purse
for the meat, he stays in the kissing posture, his eyes
rolling around to mine. "Get me out of this,"
I think he says. She lays the meat on the floor,
and he stares at it and then looks at the wall.
"Don't worry 'bout the floor, baby," she says.
"That's what I'm here for. Lie down and eat."
When was the last time I kissed a dog?
I think, and of course it all comes back. I kissed
my first several thin-lipped dogs,
my own dogs, my puppies, fuzzy sweet
mouths, licking me, generous, eyes and ears,
and my mother somewhere else and no washing.
My first private love. Now, though I have read
that dogs' mouths have fewer germs than mine,
I think, *Fewer, but maybe worse,* and I
cannot go beyond touching my nose to the dog's.
"Maybe his mother told him not to kiss people,"
I say to Edna. "He's shy and serious,"

she says. Zachary, hearing the voices, lies down
and eats the scraps. "I got a dog home,"
she says. "My old man says I'm crazy. But I,
I don't know where I could get anything better."

Grace by Valerie Shaff

BLACK DOG, RIVER, MOON

REYES GARCIA

I had a huge black dog then. She was still a child, full of trust and a feeling for adventure. Very late on a night close to the end of my irrigating summer, it rained more than ever that season. The black dog and I and a small bottle of whiskey had to go to the big headgate on the Rio so I could close off the water. The lane through the trees between my elder brother's house and mine was flooding. It was a black night, and everywhere in the dark green meadows there was water.

It is impossible to describe the feeling of sloshing at night into the flooding of the land from a big river. The power of our own river that night made the black dog and me start running like demons into the fields of water and flowers. We began to be crazed by the sounds, then by the odors of the primordial muck brought to a climax of living pungencies by a month of soaking. I chased her under the innumerable white stars, and when I got close to her would dive, catching her back legs with my bare hands, laughing, and we would be submerged in the bittersweet, smelly waters.

In an hour we reached the headgate, beyond which the swollen river moved turgidly over the rounded stones far below, and through the high, thick *alamos*. I turned the iron wheel to lower the gate until my hands bled, then crawled down to the place where the gate's mouth fed the waters into the deep *acequia madre*. And fell into the waters, listening to them.

Black dog jumped in on top of me and I laughed as I felt the long boots slowly fill up with water and grabbed at the black dog's paws and collar in the ice cold gush. Finally, after a great struggle, she pulled us both out. The work done, the terror of the river behind us, we sloshed back through the fields like children at recess, black dog and me. She had taught me to be willing to trust in the pulse of the land in our blood.

LINES ON A DOG'S FACE

MICHAEL GESSNER

Wallace said, "What the eye beholds may be
The text of life," and in this case it is
The Springer, Cynthia, whose eyes
Are the brown corridors of vacuity,
Moral deserts where the absolute Nothing
Is, or nothing but her repetitions,
The fence line patrol, the daily quarrels
With the cat, begging always for scraps
And a nap to sleep it off, then waiting
Alert for something to be known.

Agent of operation, living primordium,
Memoir of Something clearly in her stare
Which would say only, "I have known this
For a very long time," retriever
Of the stick locked in crocodile teeth,
Living the life of the fanciful
Scenario, chasing doves, the evening
Meal, her wrinkles busily playing
Out a program, a contemporary opinion,
The repetitions that govern her earth, and mine.

THE GIFT

LOUISE GLÜCK

Lord, You may not recognize me
speaking for someone else.
I have a son. He is
so little, so ignorant.
He likes to stand
at the screen door, calling
oggie, oggie, entering
language, and sometimes
a dog will stop and come up
the walk, perhaps
accidentally. May he believe
this is not an accident?
At the screen
welcoming each beast
in love's name, Your emissary.

ROSY

LOUISE GLÜCK

When you walked in with your suitcase, leaving
the door open so the night showed
in a black square behind you, with its little stars
like nailheads, I wanted to tell you
you were like the dog that came to you by default,
on three legs: now that she is again no one's
she pursues her more durable relationships
with traffic and cold nature, as though at pains
to wound herself so that she will not heal.
She is past being taken in by kindness,
preferring wet streets: what death claims
it does not abandon.
You understand, the animal means nothing to me.

MARRIED IN THE PRESENCE OF THE LORD

ALBERT GOLDBARTH

1.
Negative proof, as in: you believe
her faithful, and she does nothing
to disprove you. You do not romp
like a puppy and bark "here! this
clinches it!" at the rise of a specific
volcano in your life, but the two
of you merely grow old together
with your hands entwined
around the little negative space
you share when the palms meet.
Of course, the dog you jointly own
makes a mess of things, but cleaning
up together you say "if it don't shit
sometimes, it ain't living."

2.
Thus to give her the opportunity
of negative proof, give opportunity.
Men wink, flex, thumb rides
and checkbooks. But you believe
in her. It is religion
not when God signs the bill
in fire across the cirrus sky but
when God doesn't, and in the still
air still the pious accept Him.
So on any given day there is no thunder
in the faucet, ocher earthquake clattering
under the cup, or any chattering messenger
birds from far lands, but just the dumb dog yelps
like crazy at the door when she comes back.

WATER PIE: TONIGHT, 12/11/72

ALBERT GOLDBARTH

Tonight the air's too dry, the vents
offsetting winter cold with the enthusiasm
of retrorockets, until we're dry-mouthed
at the blast and the rims of our nostrils
cake. And in defense we scatter water

filled pie tins through the house;
in sleep, the nose sniffs in a wedge
of water pie, as much as, or more
then, the dog laps at night. Tonight,
when I wake you, my lips burn to lick

your silhouette so that it gleams in moonlight
like halved citrus, want to stop to suck
a flower of blood to your chillest hill
this season, but then continue and touch
you with my expenditure

of this wet as uniformly as it was breathed in.
There's just enough left, a circle
in the aluminum pan, to catch the arid
moon as if it snuck to drink from a gleaming
trap at our bedside. I've no sense,

it seems, of decorum; tonight there are men
on the moon. Well, let them look
down at us if they'd like! We're all
busy, reaching as far as we can,
and perhaps this makes us brothers. I know

when I walk the dog this morning he'll piss
at every tree on the block, his way of claiming

territory with water he's taken in, no pee
in the world smelling just like his. It's
a home. And I sight the sun through his flags,

his warm waves of stink on the cold wind.

BAD DOGS

DAVID GRAHAM

for Art Stringer

None of them was ever bad, trotting
off camera for the operant morsel.

Oh yes they were bad, my childhood dogs,
crinkled pets of the family album
with their names and nicknames,
impossible as fleas how they fled
behind our green sofa, where with cunning
honed for centuries on bad blood in bone
they tore one idea from the next.

In my wallet Lassie guarded
baseball cards and a Christmas dollar—
famous photo for postage and handling,
and her weekly takes I could not show
to Dandy, Flasher, Spade, and Sniffy
who knew nothing better than our smell
and put nose prints on our birdbrain windows.

Yes, worse than brutal fun, how
my dogged brother and I harnessed
our bikes with paired spaniels to pull
our weight at a stern word. Yukon King
reran five hundred Saturdays his limited
missions. We invented trials no hero
would fathom—baby dresses, grapes

soaked in gravy, sticks pantomimed
into the snapping air. They saved us
from something human, how they refused

breeding to our silly pedigrees,
and at the merest chirp of birdsong
harried in unison the flushing weeds
like brutal, exuberant owners.

HER PET

THOM GUNN

I walk the floor, read, watch a cop-show, drink,
Hear busses heave uphill through drizzling fog,
Then turn back to the pictured book to think
Of Valentine Balbiani and her dog:
She is reclining, reading, on her tomb;
But pounced, it tries to intercept her look,
Its front paws on her lap, as in this room
The cat attempts to nose beneath my book.

Her curls tight, breasts held by her bodice high,
Ruff crisp, mouth calm, hands long and delicate,
All in the pause of marble signify
A strength so lavish she can limit it.
She will not let her pet dog catch her eye
For dignity, and for a touch of wit.

Below, from the same tomb, is reproduced
A side-relief, in which she reappears
Without her dog, and everything is loosed—
Her hair down from the secret of her ears,
Her big ears, and her creased face genderless
Craning from sinewy throat. Death is so plain!
Her breasts are low knobs through the unbound dress.
In the worked features I can read the pain
She went through to get here, to shake it all,
Thinking at first that her full nimble strength
Hid like a little dog within recall,
Till to think so, she knew, was to pretend
And, hope dismissed, she sought out pain at length
And labored with it to bring on its end.

GETTING RID OF THE DOG BY TAKING IT AROUND THE MOUNTAIN

RACHEL HADAS

Swoop over rainless land.
Twin hawks circle the bay.
Driving around the mountain to give the dog away
light multiplied by sea daunts eyes like mine,
my gaze turns inland. Stony fields, ripe olives
parched on the trees, red rocks should give relief.
No, light alone, so clearly etched, inhuman,
maybe god's anger. Two tears, only water
in this bone island, wet my cheeks,
Patroklos watches in the mirror,
the dog huffs in the trunk,
going around the mountain to be given.

Peel life then to this core:
stone mountain huge awhile and beautiful
those years it was the focus of our world,
landmark for ships or swimmers headed home.
Mere rock-hump now against the span of sky,
inscrutable in overwhelming light,
still it's the magnet for our final journey.

Poor hills we pass. I wish they could be watered
with the wringing out of what has happened here
so not one drop would be wasted.
May this trip prove fruitful
and the dog be happy
on the far side of the mountain.

LAZY SLEEPING DOGS

SIDNEY HALL JR.

There are lazy
Sleeping dogs all over
My house, and they
Won't get up, they

Won't eat, won't even
Raise their noses up
To smell their own
Farts.

I would like to kick them,
But I am not the
Type to do that.
I don't know how they manage to keep

Their lives, their hair, their
Eyes, their very flatulence,
Without a bite to eat of
What I keep feeding them.

SANDRA: AT THE BEAVER TRAP

MICHAEL S. HARPER

1.
Nose only above water;
an hour in the ice melt;
paw in a beaver trap,
northern leaping through—
the outlet sieving, setter-
retriever staked to her trip,
The stake of her young
life run to nose level.

Farmers adjacent to the lake
call 'round for the owner;
at least they call around.
And a man in a pickup
pulls her out, her crushed
paw limp in the blazing sun.

Shivering on our pantry floor,
wrapped in a snowsuit,
I see her dam the clamped paw
staked to the sleeve,
licking for breaks,
a light trickle of blood
spilling from a torn nail.

2.
Next spring she will tramp
down our wire,
stamp on six goslings,
swim for teal,
run down blackbirds,
drag deer bones in our garden.

She limps on the compost pile,
shakes at the vet,
fishes under makeshift docks,
ferrets out mink,
frog, green snake,
any animal scrimmage without stakes:
listen to her spayed name—
warned, thwarted, disregarded, beautiful—
last of her line.

THIS TREE

WILLIAM HATHAWAY

said the little plaque in sober brass,
"replacing the beloved 'stump'
is a gift from the Class
of 1977." Clearly a playful crowd,
and the tree is a ginkgo, coy fans
all aflutter, already heliotroping
hard to the east. Stump hell,
I remember that old elm,
stemming higher than slate roofs
to open wide to the sky full
of God. Before they all
got dutched. Well, to this tree
someone has tethered a half-grown
spaniel bitch with vinyl clothes-
line and gone off, to class
I guess. The black pool
on gray asphalt, thick drool
roping from her sweating tongue,
mirrored a ghostly flit
of shadows from those waving
leaves. Far away her steady bark,
like a handsaw's cry as it comes
and goes through cheap pine,
or that hammer we hear
wedging air with an anger
without heat, annoyed me.
For small dogs disgust me,
yet to let loose one so young
to lose herself would be
a cruel as to tie her in the sun.
I didn't think hard

for anyone before I retied
her in some scanty locust shade.
I was sweating and panting
and probably blushing all red
and stupid, holding the styrofoam
plate of water like a choirboy
and it still sloshed anyway
on the stairs and worn tiles
before the doors of a "Job Fair"
where the kids were all three-
pieced and talcumed, holding
big brown portfolios
and getting the hell away
from my spill and red face
and kneeworn corduroy smelling
of loss and sick dog.
But I thought two small thoughts
watching the puppy shlup-shlup
it up. My dad was born (1909)
the year the chestnuts died.
Cow that is, not horse. The ones
you can eat. Also how very much
I'd like to beat the shit
out of the smug prick or princess
who left this dog tied to that tree
in the full heat of this sun.
Because, I guess after all these
trees and stumps, which I never
thought to love, I'm still
not civil. In fact, probably
only lethargy and technical
boneheadedness keeps me
from mounting the famous clocktower's
winding stairs with a trombone
case full of grief. Ah hell,
I won't hurt anyone; it's just
a little hard here in this future
with its new trees and the sun

so bright my eyes water. I'll
tell you though: take all the trees,
I'll never love a god damn stump.

LAMENT FOR THE FEET

H. L. HIX

Except a six-year pony penned from birth
Inside a barn, I never seen anything worse.
Eleven dobermans and mixed breeds, some still pups,
Removed from a residence after anonymous tips
About a dead dog decomposing on the porch.
Still and yet, this many dogs almost beats that one horse.
The problem of human freedom one might couch
In other terms than Kant's. *It's nasty in there.*
Dog shit everywhere. I don't see how she could breathe.
The woman, nearly ninety, wept and pleaded
With the workers. *I've been raising dogs right here*
In this very house since before your mothers were born.
If I'm treating these dogs as bad as you say,
How come you need those chokers to drag them away?
The Humane Society truck's radio, left on,
Played "Me and Bobby McGee." *They were strays, unwanted.*
I fed them and gave them a home. Now you'll kill them
And call me cruel. And who will protect me?
How will I sleep? When asked, the welfare worker
Said the woman cannot be forced from her home.
But freedom of will is not freedom from necessity
And obligation. The neighbors lost interest soon
And left her lawn. Meanwhile a breeze blows in
From the Gulf on a girl showing her friends the spot where
She lost her left foot to a shark. *He kept twisting it*
Like a dog with a rag, she says just to hear them squeal.
Really, he only managed to take a chunk and maul
The rest, but the doctors had to amputate.
She had to learn to trust loss. And in Houston
A boy tries to jimmy a padlock with a broom
To free his six-year-old sister from the storage shed
Their parents told them was 'the naughty room.'

She was causing trouble at school, wetting her bed,
And threatening to run away. We made a decision.
We thought a few hours here was best for her.
Police said the girl had been left water.
A person may purchase the wind and the sun
At the price of perpetual peregrination.

BEAR FAT

LINDA HOGAN

When the old man rubbed my back
with bear fat
I dreamed the winter horses
had eaten the bark off trees
and the tails of one another.

I slept a hole into my own hunger
that once ate lard and bread
from a skillet seasoned with salt.

Fat was the light
I saw through
the eyes of the bear
three bony dogs leading men
into the grass-lined cave of sleep
to kill hunger
as it slept itself thin.

They grew fat
with the swallowed grease.
they ate even the wood ashes
after the fire died
and when they slept,
did they remember back
to when they were wolves?

I am afraid of the future
as if I am the bear
turned in the stomach
of needy men
or the wolf become a dog
that will turn against itself

remembering what wildness was
before the crack of a gun,
before the men tried to kill it
or tame it
or tried to make it love them.

PYGMY HUT

ANSELM HOLLO

Heavy drops
fell from the trees
& made a
plopping
sound
as they hit
the poodles

(shouldn't that be 'puddles'

(no
not puddles
poodles

Heavy drops
fell from the trees
& made a
plopping
sound
as they hit
the poodles

This is a sort of a French poem. It has, how do you say, l'espace.

///

from SOME WORLDS

ANSELM HOLLO

once in kairouan, south of tunis, a yellow kabyle dog bit me. it was
the first time in my life, & i decided that he was right. he was simply
expressing, in his own way, that i was in the wrong.

                                        thus rainer
maria rilke, in a letter to a friend. this rilke was a man who loved
dogs & had a profound understanding of them. one of his sonnets to
orpheus is not addressed to orpheus at all, but to a dog. it deplores
the difficulties of communication between men & dogs, & i wish i
could say (now, half a century later) that those problems have been
solved, or that these very words are in fact written by a dog. but that
would be telling a lie, & should a dog read this at some time in the
future, he or she would immediately recognize it as such.

ON THE DOG ANGEL

MIROSLAV HOLUB

False tears of light on macadam.
Maybe he was thinking of a bitch
or remembering a bone—
knives or evil-eyed wheels
caught and cut and crushed—

his jaw's dislocated, he
crawls off, yelps—no!
yelps, falls, whimpers
and lies still.

People around
see:
the dog angel,
shaggy and black
with muddy wings
and the huge pain
spreading its halo
over the puddles.

Darkness
wrings its hands
over the body and sound
columns to the sky.
They drag him
out of the way.

Just a rag,
a graveyard rag,
nothing more.

The angel's
on the roof,
sniffing the chimney,
gnawing the bones of shooting stars.

LIKE FEELINGS

CHRISTOPHER HOWELL

Moonlight is all over the sycamores
and down the street singing
like a drunk.
It's all over my dog and me, too,
stepping out our evening's amble
among the crickets and parked cars,
couples murmuring on porch swings.
It is fifteen years
we've been doing this,
walking the night streets
pleasantly fried by dreams lifting
everywhere along the tall boughs,
and it is inside us now
like feelings
that bloom open as we move
so that finally we are out of reckoning,
smoothly
richly filled, like jars, with all our nights
and walks together;
and nothing spills or shatters this.

An angry shadow from an alley leaps
and stabs us
and we just step out of our bodies
and go on.
"That's life,
thank God" (mine and the god of dogs) I don't
tell him, or anyone
but you.

And I don't say I've got the pain of it
shut off or that I've buried my last

deceit. After all,
it's just the dog listening
or not
as things gleam and lumber in the rows
of darkness,
and what is there to say
to him?
I could unhinge the old
existentialist saw
about the sanctity of moments.
I could promise him a bone when we get back
then break my promise just to show
the waywardness of speech and truth.
Or I could tell him love
is like the air sometimes
and vice versa; which is to say, all there is
to live on.
But he knows that.

THIS AFTERWARD

CHRISTOPHER HOWELL

The sand in the eye-
let of a shoe is not what I want
to feel myself singing with.
And I care less for clouds
than for those marsh-lights
sparking prairie borders where there is no marsh,
where my dog and I walked so many times
admiring them anyway. And—don't
interrupt me yet—the shape of sound and dark
I need to utter is a bell, a fine silver
death bell for that dog (this whole
irreducible moment I reach into
is for him) who was my friend and now
is gone. You could hear that
if you became my life, you could hear
the silence after small bells stop
and you're just walking and walking
by yourself.

ABOUT THE DOGS OF DACHAU

RICHARD JACKSON

I'd even given you part of my shared fear:
This personal responsibility
For a whole world's disease that is our nightmare.
SIDNEY KEYES

About the hearts of dusk that could make
pets of dogs the Nazis abandoned as they fled.
About turning to answer the dust devil
scuffed up by the wind, thinking I heard your voice,
and seeing the Rottweiler rise, alarmed, from the gravel.
About the Shepherd out near the disinfecting shack
nosing decades-old scents along the inner fence.
Also, about Mr. Valincourt's Doberman,
another summer, 1956, the olive
drab coat I borrowed from my father
caught on the chain link fence where I played army.
About that lost world where I carried death
on my shoulders, where the moss on the moonlight
said nothing yet about the piles of dead shoes.
Nothing of what I want to tell you.
About the dogs clamoring at the sound of a distant train,
about the shell casings of words we wanted to forget.
About this place.
About the fragment of a mouth organ
I found along the stream that is
still crossed by barbed wire. About the way
it freezes in winter and the man caught on the wires,
1941, the museum photograph says,
a spider's pod of snow wrapping around him.
About this place.
About our love in a world where the air is swollen,
where clouds only bruise the sky,
where stars refuse to connect as constellations.
About the coats heaped in a pile at one end of the camp.
About the lice, so many they could move an empty arm,

as if each coat were alive.
About those coats you can still hear
on a camp bench, maybe looking over a makeshift
chessboard and through themselves at the tourists.
About how clean this place is. The past
trying to stay only in the past. About the unbelievable
postcards, showing collections of rings,
hair, teeth, the body's trash dump.
Why I sent you the blank card from here.
Why my terror went looking for clothes,
poking like a searchlight through rags of words.
Why I wanted to hold you until we turned into birds
because here it is only the birds that are not branded by fire,
because they can turn into specks, then stars
so distant we can never disturb their light.
About the swamp at one end of the camp,
and the town at the other where the smell must have drifted.
About no one wondering. About the cries of the dogs
interrupting the still nights in that town.
About the old questions darkening the trees of the town,
and about the old answers lighting the treetops.
About these sentences that cannot stop
at the horizon. These words with their nervous jugulars.
About everything returning, as Nietzsche threatened it would,
the pack of shadows crossing the yard like dogs,
the one turning to snarl like Mr. Valincourt's Doberman
at the coats who must stand for hours in the yard nearly naked,
at the execution procession with its slumped coats
stumbling through the mud, forced to play
the grotesque violins and trombones for their own deaths.
About this mouth organ, if that's what it is,
the rust and wood crumbling like a badly remembered song.
About how the inmates put on the night, the day,
how they put on tomorrow, the erratic flight of a butterfly
that has escaped the snapping dogs,
put on even the flowers, the trees, the windows,
how they put on the camp weather vane
which is another name for the soul.
About this tabloid I bought pointing to the frog boy,

kept alive by authorities like a huge tadpole,
peering out from his home in Peru.
About the huge coat he tries to hide in like a pod.
About wanting to kiss those eyes
bulging from his forehead, the flipper arm
reaching out as if to brush a fly. About the dogs, the town dogs
that go crazy when he is wheeled out to the yard.
About the dogs of Dachau,
how they sleep beneath the barracks like pools
of water that do not reflect the sky,
how their cries stiffen the coats and rub the eyes of morning.
About one of these coats, Esad. About the way
he slumps in his bunk, peering out like the frog boy,
the dysentery leaking from the bunks above.
About his festering foot sticking to the straw.
His experimental foot observed by the camp doctor.
About how even the starlight shakes the wind
carrying the screams from high altitude experiments,
cold water experiments, malaria experiments,
and how the echoes of the dogs sniff through
the abandoned ghettoes of the heart.
About the woman. The way, each night,
he would tremble before her in his own skin
like a cyprus whose sparrows are
stirring to leave. About skin,
about flesh, because it is so alive taking flight.
About the way he dreams us, the way the coats
in those camp photos dream someone will wonder,
decades later, who they were. About his dream of
the way I rise from you, slump to the side like he does,
and the way you cry, the way we both cry maybe
just because we can make the stars into constellations,
because we have skin to touch and to cover.
About the simple coats we put on, putting on the world.
About this small mouth organ he must have refused to play,
a few keys tuned too high at one end for the dogs.
About fashioning it out of splinters from the bunks,
of metal from the camp shop, of the sky
that shrugged above his childhood in Istria,

the broken wings he fixed, the pain
of the quarter moon afraid it couldn't go on.
About the pockets it was carried in, the old faces
that crowd onto it like a sinking boat,
to snap it against the palms of our words,
so that the leaf will not have to face its death alone,
so that the whole landscape will turn into music,
this small mouth organ, this graveyard of voices,
from which no song must ever be finished.

LIKE DOGS AT A CONCERT

STAN JAMES

Sometimes we're at our lives
The same way dogs are at a concert—
We hear all of the sounds
And none of the music.

Which is not to say all dogs
are at their lives
the way they're at a concert.
Though, these days even
some dogs are that.

THE STRAY DOG BY THE SUMMERHOUSE

DONALD JUSTICE

This morning, down
By the summerhouse,
I saw a stray,
A stray dog dead.
All white and brown
The dead friend lay,
All brown with a white
Mark on his head.
His eyes were bright
And open wide,
Bright, open eyes
With worms inside,
And the tongue hung loose
To the butterflies,
The butterflies
And the flying ants.

And because of the tongue
He seemed like one
Who has run too long,
And stops, and pants.
And because of the sun
There came a scent,
And it was strong.
It came and went
As if somewhere near
A round, ripe pear,
So ripe, so round,
Had dropped to the ground
And with the heat

Was turning black.
And the scent came back,
And it was sweet.

Jumping Dog by Elliot Erwitt (MAGNUM PHOTO)

A DOG AND A BOY

RICHARD KATROVAS

Joe Brickhouse saw his dog
get smashed by a garbage truck
in Elizabeth City, North Carolina.
He was twelve and smoked Luckies
and had a glass eye.
I won't tell you about the games of marbles
or how he fucked his sister,
nor shall I discuss in the abstract
his deep-seated contempt for authority
or why he kicked my ass
just because I was his friend and he loved me.
For this is about a dog and a boy
and has virtually nothing to do with Mark Twain
and the rest of American literature.
It's about a garbage truck
that backed up over a beautiful Lab
and a white kid who wrapped his arms
around the dead animal and gasped for air
and his face turned red then bluish,
whose tears streamed
onto the blood-caked fur of the dog,
and who howled and screamed so loud
at gray and porch-lit 5 a.m.
windows all down Merrimac scraped open,
and T-shirts, drawers, scrungy robes
hobbled onto porches
to stare in wonder
at a human being
who had learned so young
how to talk to the dead.

DOG

WELDON KEES

to Vincent Hugh

"This night is monstrous winter when the rats
Swarm in great packs along the waterfront,
When midnight closes in and takes away your name.
And it was Rover, Ginger, Laddie, Prince;
My pleasure hambones. Donned a collar once
With golden spikes, the darling of a cultured home
Somewhere between the harbor and the heights, uptown.
Or is this something curs with lathered mouths invent?
They had a little boy I would have bitten, had I dared.
They threw great bones out on the balcony.
But where? I pant at every door tonight.

I knew this city once the way I know those lights
Blinking in chains along the other side,
These streets that hold the odors of my kind.
But now, my bark's a ghost in this strange scentless air,
I am no growling cicerone or cerberus
But wreckage for the pound, snuffling in shame
All cold-nosed toward identity. — Rex? Ginger? No.
A sort of panic jabbering inside begins.
Wild for my shadow in this vacantness,
I can at least run howling toward the bankrupt lights
Into the traffic where bones, cats, and masters swarm.
And where my name must be."

Harmony Stoneworks, Late Winter

Brigit Pegeen Kelly

Sunday is silence in the pit, the gate locked,
the trucks gone, the road all mine, mine the stone wall

I sit upon that borders the field, tree-locked
and locked within a larger field. This is where

the spaniel comes, where the alleys of stubble fill
with darkness and wash him toward me—one-eyed spaniel,

filthy, wearing his patched body like a madman's coat
as he runs up one side of the wall and down the other.

Why does he cross this field of stones and cold, of
sodden cobs the reaper dropped, where the hackberries

wrestle to bring forth new leaves? Why does he run
this ring around me? O spaniel, mad spaniel,

are you lost to the whistle, wet in your master's mouth,
too high-pitched or too remote for my ears, calling you

North, calling you South? Or lost to your small heart
telling you cross, cross space and you will own it?

The swallows build the bank. Are you my fear?
Blind as the wind that works to pull their nets down?

DOG

BRIGIT PEGEEN KELLY

When you first felt the foul dog walking
up the corn row of your spine, you remembered
walking by the soy fields down the long road
to the limestone quarry, remembered the trucks
lumbering and how the mind shuts its gates
and called down a sort of sleep to keep
the trucks' roar back. You rode that sound
without resistance, like a boat upon
the working waves, while as each diesel passed
the dog leapt and fought like a fish on the chain
by your side.
                What walks inside walks outside.
Death has a thousand pictures in the world.
You lie and worms eat the oak, you steal
bread and an old woman riddled with
superstitions drops her mirror and weakens
to the loss of luck. There was another dog.
The gentle mongrel given to you
as a gift and hit one day by a truck.
It died slowly on a heap of rags in the shed,
its back legs crushed, soiling itself
as it tried to rise, and howling, howling.
There was the smell of urine and cold cement,
of winter trees and of the snow
that the wind carried in as a biting spray,
while the birds dropped their calls
in the woods. And because the smells
frightened you and the way the dog threw back
his head and would not listen, and how
his eyes, yellowed with pain, would not see,
and how in his head he cried he went on
walking, walking, wherever it was he walked,

you kicked him to stop the noise,
kicked and kicked, as if you were kicking
the loud wheel of the truck that stuck him,
as if you were that wheel itself, raising
a churning wave of snow and then,
like time, rolling over the hill
and never coming back.
                              The dog died.
You ate your meals and said your prayers.
Your life was a life. But now where you sit
at your desk overlooking the wet fields
something scratches at the base of your neck
and pulls your head up, so that you see coming
toward you with dead calm through the dusk
a forest—dark and limbless.

TAFFY

MARY KINZIE

We were tired of the Easter chicks
Grown scruffy, rabbits hopping above their scat,
  Molting parrots feisty as gin
    With soda mixed in,
    Warrens to restraw,
Then the collie came and swept away all that:
  Fading in swiftness, fetching sticks,
  She moved us like a natural law.

  She was everybody's dog, yet when
I spoke to her, she came. Her friendliness
  Drew light down on the neighborhood.
    Nothing but good
    Streamed from her—smartness, repose,
The gaiety of some higher creature's dress
  Worn obligingly—and then
  We saw the visitation close.

  After her, our interest waned.
The family as a whole thought better of
  The start up of the old routine,
    Cages to clean,
  Housebreaking, food, the vet,
Which she had made us, in access of love
  For one whose forthright being pained
  Us to remember, once forget.

CUSTODIAN

MAXINE KUMIN

Every spring when the ice goes out
black commas come scribbling across the shallows.
Soon they sprout forelegs.
Slowly they absorb their tails
and by mid-June, full-voiced, announce themselves.

Enter our spotted dog.
Every summer, tense with the scent of them,
tail arced like a pointer's but wagging
in anticipation, he stalks his frogs
two hundred yards clockwise around
the perimeter of this mucky pond,
then counterclockwise, an old pensioner
happy in his work.

Once every ten or so pounces
he succeeds, carries his captive north
in his soft mouth, uncorks him on the grass,
and then sits, head cocked, watching the slightly
dazed amphibian hop back to sanctuary.

Over the years the pond's inhabitants
seem to have grown accustomed
to this ritual of capture and release.
They ride untroubled in the wet pocket
of the dog's mouth, disembark in the meadow
like hitchhikers, and strike out again for home.

I have seen others of his species kill
and swallow their catch and then be seized
with violent retchings. I have seen children
corner polliwogs in the sun-flecked hollow

by the green rock and lovingly squeeze
the life out of them in their small fists.
I have seen the great blue heron swoop in
time after wing-slapping time to carry
frogs back to the fledglings in the rookery.

Nothing is to be said here
of need or desire. No moral arises
nor is this, probably, purgatory.
We have this old dog,
custodian of an ancient race of frogs,
doing what he knows how to do
and we too, taking and letting go,
that same story.

WHERE THE DOGS LIE DOWN WITH THE CATS

GREG KUZMA

for Claire Hill

The old enmity
does not apply.
The maple tree
lets down its waterfall
of seeds
to whirl and swirl
onto the porch
where the cats play
and the dog sleeps.
Now the kitten of
many colors
whose fur resembles
a bag of assorted marbles
brown and black and orange and white
leaps for the tabletop
or climbs with claws
into wicker
the table leg.
It is protected by its
innocence.
The flag that flies
above this fortress
is white.
We have surrendered here
to love and letting live
each creature as itself.
Even the spider
having spun her intricate web
upon the porch's awning stripes
is spared to spin again

in the bush beside the porch—
where I am writing this,
where even the poet is safe.

THE RETURN

GREG KUZMA

Upon reaching home I wrote this poem sitting in the car.

> The miles are behind me now
> and whatever is new for me yet
> I have come home.
> I do not care if the trumpets blow.

We have a small shed in the yard, and then the light struck it in a particular way.

> Oh shed, I cried,
> what can you tell the sun
> in whose light you are now bathed
> and beautiful.

It was my custom to come directly into the house, but this day the air smelled of the rain we had just last night had, and so I decided to walk about among the trees. The white dog, whose body is fat, emerged from out of a bush beside the path, and this poem leapt from me.

> What do we tell the ones we love.
> How do we come to them.
> How does the flower share its beauty.
> And now the white dog is beside me,
> I who have done nothing all day
> but pass the tar of the road
> under my wheels.

After dinner I went out alone under the stars.

> And I saw them, still speaking to me.
> And the owl sang.

There was a dead mouse still in its trap where one of the children had
left it beside the garbage can. Its eyes bulged black. Other details
came to my attention. I saw how the body lay flat and the tail was slack.
But what could I say of it that has not been written. Still I must write my
poem.

It is winter and the houses are warm.
They are great pumpkins aglow with heat.
From all over the creatures come,
and many are nuisances and must be destroyed.

I slept fitfully all the night, hearing sounds, and there was a branch
scratching the window. Once, in a dream, my mother's hand came
at me, but then turned into the branch scratching the window. I woke,
as I had been, a child, homeless, with only my breath for company.

Oh deep green sea of night,
I have sailed on you, obedient and calm,
and even your storms have not afrighted me.
But when, oh when, will I sense shore,
smell the ripe fruit so delicious
which grows only where your waves break.

Snow has fallen.

The hands of the snow bear messages.
They are about ecstasy, and sleep.
Melt as we read them.

When I had dressed I descended the steps. I felt like an old old man,
who, rising, goes down and out among his dogs. He lays his hands
on them, they shiver, and then he scatters the food for them. No breath
is taken, there is no thought for the self all the morning.

At the back door, pieces of earth,
wind, the snow heaped,
and the three dogs holding their breaths.
I move among them singing.

We moved together out through the snow. The smaller one was almost
covered in the drifts. At last I picked her up, felt her wild heart.
And the cold pierced us like angry eyes.

> Keep what you have, men with gold earrings,
> and in your pockets gold.
> He who has dogs has enough.

We stopped our travel and sat by an old fence.

> Where do you go now wood and wire
> the earth all owned.
> Wind and rain have taken the face
> from his bent post.

At last my thoughts turned homeward. The wind had ceased, and the
sun shone brightly. We turned at an old bridge, in order to retrace
our steps. We had gone far out beyond the houses. I looked about me,
surprised, as I am always surprised by vigor, and by the litter men
have made of the good land. To speak unto my dogs, but could they
hear me, is my intent in this poem.

> See we have come far
> past bankers past the bakers house.
> Black dog I love you
> who owns no objects.

THE WRONG WAY WILL HAUNT YOU (SHOOTING A HOUND)

SYDNEY LEA

Spittle beads as ice along
her jaw on this last winter day.
And when I lift her, all her bones
are loose and light as sprigs of hay.

For years her wail has cut the woods
in parts, familiar. Hosts of hares
have glanced behind as she plowed on
and pushed them to me unawares.

Now her muzzle skims the earth
as if she breathed a far dim scent,
and yet she holds her tracks to suit
my final, difficult intent.

For years with gun in hand I sensed
her circle shrinking to my point.
How odd that ever I should be
the center to that whirling hunt.

Here a yip and there a chop
meant some prime buck still blessed with breath,
and in the silences I feared
she'd run him to her own cold death.

The snow that clouds my sights could be
a trailing snow, just wet and new
enough to keep a scent alive,
but not so deep that she'd fall through.

She falls without a sound. Her blood
runs circular upon the ground.

I lug her to those thick strange woods
where she put our first hare around.

I kick a drift-top over her
(the hardpan won't accept my spade).
The wind makes up a howl as in
all cold old ballads on The Grave.

INSTRUCTIONS: THE DOG (RAY SPEAKS)

SYDNEY LEA

He's not a pet, not meant to be.
Keep him outdoors in a well-built pen, roofed over.
A roofless pen won't hold a natural hunter.
He'll look you in the eye for longer than just any
dog when you look at him. When he's a pup,
just let him go, just let him chase. You'll let him
know birds are his business. You want it so
you might as well call that birch tree as him
when he's got his nose in something. If he's smart
he'll teach himself to quarter, hunt the wind,
and slow so as not to bump the birds. At last
he'll point. He has an instinct. Understand,
respect it, feel it. Don't give a lot of orders.
Be in shape. Keep up. Don't make him wait.
A bird will sit for just so long, and he
will know—if he's worth keeping—better far
than you *how* long. Be sure before you shoot
in the early months. He needs to find a thread
among the point, the flush, the shot. Dead bird.
If he wants to, let him chew the first ones up.
Get him all excited for a bird.
You'll find another. Watch the feathers burst
up in the breeze. He'll hurt the bird much less
than you imagine. Stand right still in honor
of the point from time to time: a front leg lifted,
nose a-quiver, eyes unblinking. All
that concentration of the senses! Then walk in,
excited, heart still pounding after all
the years and kills, the autumn air still tangy
to a poor man's scent, the bird in there somewhere
thinking a quick route out of sight.
And if you swing the gun too fast or slow

you will not eat. Be careful. These aren't practice rounds.
And when he dies, you get him quickly,
quickly as a man can make it, in the ground.

Dogs Looking at Dogs by Misha Erwitt (MAGNUM PHOTO)

THE DOG OF ART

DENISE LEVERTOV

The dog with daisies for eyes
who flashes forth
flame of his very self at every bark
is the Dog of Art.
Worked in wool, his blind eyes
look inward to caverns of jewels
which they see perfectly,
and his voice
measures forth the treasure
in music sharp and loud,
sharp and bright,
bright flaming barks,
and growling smoky soft, the Dog
of Art turns to the world
the quietness of his eyes.

DOG POEM

PHILIP LEVINE

Fierce and stupid all dogs are
and some worse. I learned this
early by walking to school
unarmed and unprepared
for big city life, which they
had been bred to for centuries.
The chow who barred my way
snarling through his black lips
taught me I was tiny and helpless
and that if he grew more determined
I could neither talk nor fight,
and my school books, my starred exams,
my hand-woven woolen mittens, a gift
of my grandmother, would fall
to the puddled sidewalk and
at best my cold sack of lunch
might buy me a few moments
to prepare my soul before I slept.
I inched by him, smelling the breath
hot and sour as old clothes.
He did nothing but rave, rising
toward me on his hind legs
and choking against the collar
which miraculously held. Later,
years later, delivering mail
on bicycle in the new California,
I was set on by a four-footed moron
who tore at my trousers even
as I drummed small rocks off
his head. I dreamed that head
became soup, and the small eyes stared
out into the bright dining room

of the world's great dog lovers,
and they ate and wept by turns
while I pedaled through the quiet streets
bringing bad news and good to
the dogless citizenry of Palo Alto.
The shepherd dog without sheep
who guards the gates to sleep wakens
each night as my tiny boat
begins to drift out on the waters
of silence. He bays and bays
until the lights come on, and I
sit up sweating and alarmed, alone
in the bed I came to call home.
Now I am weary of fighting and carry
at all times small hard wafers
of dried essence of cat to purchase
a safe way among the fanged masters
of the avenues. If I must come back
to this world let me do so as the lion
of legend, but striped like an alley cat.
Let me saunter back the exact way
I came turning each corner to face
the barking hosts of earth until they
scurry for cover or try pathetically
to climb the very trees that earlier
they peed upon and shamed. Let their pads
slide upon the glassy trunks,
weight them down with exercise books,
sacks of postcards, junk mail, ads,
dirty magazines, give them three kids
in the public schools, hemorrhoids,
a tiny fading hope to rise above
the power of unleashed, famished animals
and postmasters, give them two big feet
and shoes that don't fit, and dull work
five days a week. Give them my life.

So You Put the Dog to Sleep

Thomas Lux

I have no dog, but it must be
Somewhere there's one belongs to me.
John Kendrick Bangs

You love your dog and carve his steaks
(marbled, tender, aged) in the shape of hearts.
You let him on your lap at will.

and call him by a lover's name: *Liebchen*,
pooch-o-mine, lamby, honey-tart,
and fill your voice with tenderness, woo.

He loves you too, that's his only job,
it's how he pays his room and board.
Behind his devotion, though, his dopey looks,

might be a beast who wants your house,
your wife; who in fact loathes you, his lord.
His jaws snapping while asleep means dreams

of eating your face: nose, lips, eyebrows, ears . . .
But soon your dog gets old, his legs
go bad, he's nearly blind, you purée his meat

and feed him with a spoon. It's hard to say
who hates whom the most. He will not beg.
So you put the dog to sleep. Bad dog.

THE MONGREL DOG AND I

THOMAS MCAFEE

Frank, the mongrel dog, and I—
we have mange together. I with
my dandruff and flaking face,
Frank with his thinning hair and sores.
    —Old wanderer, dear tramp, and evil-smelling
wagger-of-tail, he almost blesses me
when I break out the canned horse meat.
    But I am Frank's defeat.
The mange won't cure: I kill him.
    Who is my defeat? To give me
mercy I don't want.

A METAPHOR CROSSES THE ROAD

MARTHA MCFERREN

Sometimes super cool
is nothing more than
pure preparedness.
Like my friend Janet
who was terrified
someday she'd swerve
to miss a dog
and demolish her car
and kill herself
and maybe her children.
For years, whenever
she got behind a wheel
she was thinking,
Hit the dog, hit the dog,
and finally one night
the dog got there
and she slammed
flat across him.

I cried real tears
when Lassie came home,
but I'm worth something, too.
Let's both watch out, dog.

In August

Thomas McGrath

Sultry afternoon. The old dog
Moves his fleas under the porch.
Instantly light crackles
Ahead of the rattling linestorm.

THE DOG IN THE BAR-ROOM MIRROR

FREYA MANFRED

Unexpectedly a mirror reveals me
as I am, a country hick, pure ham
and potato spuds and beer. Unabashed
the toothy grin stands forth, and
the large breasted body and the childish chin.
Compose yourself, I say, this is not
the best day on record as the Almanac (Farmer's)
and the faces on the bar have said. Joy is dead.
But beside me in the mirror a friendly dog
steps forth, rollicking the tiled floor,
nearly unhinging the door with glee. Flapping
ears hang free. This is me?
Restrict that giggle, you. There's no
room for a wiggler in your booth. It's uncouth.
Go back to where you sit with teachers
drear and fat debating their first drink.
I turn to go, but first I bend
to give myself a quick, consoling pat.

LINES I TOLD MYSELF I WOULDN'T WRITE

PAUL MARIANI

Nebuchadnezzar, von Hoffman the Great, then
Big Sur and Paterson. Instead: since it was
really my kid's dog, we settled for Sparky.
Better than Killer, I guess, better than

White Fang. An onomastic gesture if ever
there was one, more in line with the Ford
pickups sloped to the sides before the town's
one beerstop. And what with Argentine

conscripts freezing in Darwin and her Majesty's
soldiers leapfrogging the Falklands
out of San Carlo, the *Belgrano* gone
and the *Sheffield* a grave, I promised

myself I wouldn't get soft over one fleabag
arthritic half gone in the head when he didn't
come home. Springtime, we figured, and the old
prunewrinkled groinbag out after women

over in Leverett or up by the lake. But as day
followed day, then a week, then a month,
and his cracked greasy bowl got sacked first
by a tom then by two cranky jays. . . .

There were three nights in there when my wife
kept waking me up, hearing him with each shift
in the wind, and she'd sit up in bed, listening,
the same way she did whenever one of the babies

got stuck in their breathing. I know I said
I wouldn't go weepy when the time came, and I haven't.

At least not that much. And besides, half the neighbors
must be doing the two-step, and the kid who delivers

the papers and used to fling them into the bushes
whenever he heard Sparky can breathe easier now.
And last week a friend put the whole thing
in its proper perspective, reminding me how in Taiwan

and places like that they serve them as delicacies.
So it's over and done with: the backyard service,
the young dogwood planted. Except for the dream,
where an old dog, battered and nettle-flecked, limps

down to the river. Across its wide waters he sniffs
till he sees us. And at first he shudders,
he knows he must plunge in. When he springs forth
his red coat glistens. His tail whacks

back and forth, back and forth. As in an Aztec
mound painting caught in the flickering gleam
of the torch, the eyes shift, blend into one.
The lips have curled up. The bright eye shines.

LANDSCAPE WITH DOG

PAUL MARIANI

Often up the back steps he came
bearing gifts: frozen squirrels,
sodden links of sausage, garter snakes,
the odd sneaker. The gnarled marks
are still there as witness to that,
confined, he took his tensions out
on doors & tables. And life went on,
& mornings, peace & war, good times
& depressions. Pale sticks turned
to trees, boys to larger boys, then men.
Ice storms, wakes, elections came & went.
And always he was there, like air,
a good wife. But then there's this
to think about & think about again:

the last time I saw Sparky he was dying.
His legs trembled & he kept moping
after me. I remember trying to get
my stubborn mower started, with no time
then to stop & pet a dog. And having
no time left himself, Sparky
thanked me in the only way he could
for eleven years of care, then got up
& walked out of my life & lay down
somewhere in the woods to die,
one of the best things life ever
handed me, while I went on looking
for a one-inch nut & bolt
in among my rusting odds & ends.

HOMER'S SEEING-EYE DOG

WILLIAM MATTHEWS

Most of the time he wrote, a sort of sleep
with a purpose, so far as I could tell.
How he got from the dark of sleep
to the dark of waking up I'll never know;
the lax sprawl sleep allowed him
began to set from the edges in,
like a custard, and then he was awake—
me too, of course, wriggling my ears
while he unlocked his bladder and stream
of dopey wake-up jokes. The one
about the wine-dark pee I hated instantly.
I stood at the ready, like a god
in an epic, but there was never much
to do. Oh, now and then I'd make a sure
intervention, save a life, whatever.
But my exploits don't interest you,
and of his life all I can say is that
when he'd poured out his work
the best of it was gone and then he died.
He was a great man and I loved him.
Not a whimper about his sex life—
how I detest your prurience—
but here's a farewell literary tip:
I myself am the model for Penelope.
Don't snicker, you hairless moron,
I know so well what "faithful" means
there's not even a word for it in Dog.
I just embody it. I think you bipeds
have a catchphrase for it: "To thine own self
be true, . . ." though like a blind man's shadow,

the second half is only there for those who know
it's missing. Merely a dog, I'll tell you
what it is: "... as if you had a choice."

LOYAL

WILLIAM MATTHEWS

They gave him an overdose
of anesthetic, and its fog
shut down his heart in seconds.
I tried to hold him, but he was
somewhere else. For so much of love
one of the principals is missing,
it's no wonder we confuse love
with longing. Oh I was thick
with both. I wanted my dog
to live forever and while I was
working on impossibilities
I wanted to live forever, too.
I wanted company and to be alone.
I wanted to know how they trash
a stiff ninety-five pound dog
and I paid them to do it
and not tell me. What else?
I wanted a letter of apology
delivered by a decrepit hand,
by someone shattered for each time
I'd had to eat pure pain. I wanted
to weep, not "like a baby,"
in gulps and breath-stretching
howls, but steadily, like an adult,
according to the fiction
that there is work to be done,
and almost inconsolably.

THE VICTOR DOG

JAMES MERRILL

for Elizabeth Bishop

Bix to Buxtehude to Boulez,
The little white dog on the Victor label
Listens long and hard as he is able.
It's all in a day's work, whatever plays.

From judgment, it would seem, he has refrained.
He even listens earnestly to Bloch,
Then builds a church upon our acid rock.
He's man's—no—he's the Leiermann's best friend,

Or would be if hearing and listening were the same.
Does he hear? I fancy he rather smells
Those lemon-gold arpeggios in Ravel's
"Les jets d'eau du palais de ceux qui s'aiment."

He ponders the Schumann Concerto's tall willow hit
By lightning, and stays put. When he surmises
Through one of Bach's eternal boxwood mazes
The oboe pungent as a bitch in heat,

Or when the calypso decants its raw bay rum
Or the moon in *Wozzeck* reddens ripe for murder,
He doesn't sneeze or howl; just listens harder.
Adamant needles bear down on him from

Whirling of outer space, too black too near—
But he was taught as a puppy not to flinch,
Much less to imitate his bête noire Blanche
Who barked, fat foolish creature, at King Lear.

Still others fought in the road's filth over Jezebel,
Slavered on hearths of horned and pelted barons.

His forebears lacked, to say the least, forbearance.
Can nature change in him? Nothing's impossible.

The last chord fades. The night is cold and fine.
His master's voice rasps through the grooves' bare groves.
Obediently, in silence like the grave's
He sleeps there on the still-warm gramophone.

Only to dream he is at the première of a Handel
Opera long thought lost—*Il Cane Minore*.
Its allegorical subject is his story!
A little dog revolving round a spindle

Gives rise to harmonies beyond belief,
A cast of stars. . . . Is there in Victor's heart
No honey for the vanquished? Art is art.
The life it asks of us is a dog's life.

ALI

W. S. MERWIN

Small dog named for a wing
never old and never young

abandoned with your brothers on a beach
when you were scarcely weaned

taken home starving
by one woman with
too many to feed as it was

handed over to another
who tied you out back in the weeds
with a clothesline and fed you if she remembered

on the morning before the eclipse of the moon
I first heard about you over the telephone

only the swellings of insect bites
by then held the skin away from your bones

thin hair matted filthy the color of mud
naked belly crusted with sores
head low frightened silent watching

I carried you home and gave you milk and food
bathed you and dried you

dressed your sores and sat with you
in the sun with your wet head on my leg

we had one brother of yours already
and had named him for the great tree of the islands

we named you for the white shadows
behind your thin shoulders

and for the remainder of the desert
in your black muzzle lean as an Afghan's
and for the lightness of your ways
not the famished insubstance of your limbs

but even in your sickness and weakness
when you were hobbles with pain and exhaustion

an aerial grace a fine buoyancy
a lifting as in the moment before flight

I keep finding why that is your name

the plump vet was not impressed with you
and guessed wrong for a long time
about what was the matter

so that you could hardly eat
and never grew like your brother

small dog wise in your days

never servile never disobediant
and never far

standing with one foot on the bottom stair
hoping it was bedtime

standing in the doorway looking up
tail swinging slowly below sharp hip bones

toward the end you were with us whatever we did

the gasping breath through the night
ended an hour and a half before daylight

the gray tongue hung from your mouth
we went on calling you holding you

feeling the sudden height

ELEPHANT, DOG, RIVER

GILES MITCHELL

I have walked and prayed
Because of the great gloom
that is in my mind.
YEATS

When I was a boy, proud small-molded ministers
who had seen as little of deity
as maybe a single holy eyelash or pointed finger,
warned us about an unpardonable sin
they didn't define, being distraught before
their twisting mirrors,
                so now in old age
I tell people the truth about my animals.
A recent documentary reported the waning
of the long day of the elephant
and prophesied with awful accuracy
that when the last elephant was gone
life would be more barren and cruel—
I sleep so little I seem to have conjunctivitis
all over my face. I stumblebum far into the nights
searching the sterile dark.

I've never really had a dog.
They've never liked me much; they've either run off
or preferred somebody else.
Once I wanted one so bad I tried
the kind that wears pink ribbons and bows.
She wouldn't even stay in the same room where I was,
much less sleep at my feet.
I'd always thought hounds weren't particular,
just wanted a shady place, fairly regular food
and a pat on the head sometimes,
but I was all wrong. Of that,
Sarah's St. Bernard seemed especially aware.

What I finally got was an elephant
when Sarah and I were camping on
the Colorado River above Austin near Bend.
All weekend, with abandoning her on my mind
and finding myself a younger woman,
I'd glimpsed him several times.
Suddenly he faced me close up, flecked with dim
ceremonial blue processional paint, hierophantic,
extended trunk almost touching my forehead.
Nearby, Sarah was looking for pretty rocks, keepers.
As I tensed my heart to leave her
the elephant turned from me
and plunged into the foam,
going under as if committing suicide.
Sarah hadn't seen the animal
but when she heard the sinking sound
the look in her gray, Athena eyes
must have made Hades howl with grief
and me mad with hidden regret.

When he came back years later, diminished,
a gorgeous, frigid girl I was seeing
spent the night, and his right tusk disappeared.
He asked me to look at him, then departed.
Months later he returned, nervous
but still seemed to belong
and I rode him through a narrow street
crowded with strangers. That time I was alone
unless you count the Baptist church
I was guiding him into, when an explosion
at the entrance made him shiver and dissolve
until one night I awoke, my arms around his trunk.
Lying on his side facing me
a bullet hole in his forehead
I tried not to notice, he asked
why I had shot him, and I blacked out.

Then went on with my little safe life
with replicas of this wintry woman

mixing lust and fear and calling it desire,
the elephant appearing at times
like a blot shimmering on a desert
or on a bar stool.
                              Over the years
I've lied a lot about him,
saying he was only a dream totem
but implying he was my guide and mentor.
I've collected mostly inexpensive carvings
onyx, wood, pewter, one ivory (mammoth, not modern)
hoping for a fool's grace dream (i.e., unearned)
that would redeem my shame.

Sixty years old and reflecting, finally upon my doom
I allowed myself a last affair—another bored woman
ravening, her avatar a beautiful pet jaguar
that bit me badly on the back of my head
one night at her house when she was goading me
into having sex with her.
                              Maundering about
my missing elephant I did it, once, at my house.
Then after she finished her scream
                              a faint infrasonic cry
came from the living room
where on an antique table my elephant sat,
the size of a toy terrier
and still visibly shrinking.
As I leaned down to listen
to his last words, he turned to stone,
a polished granite, that vanished
while I watched.

Though I have not told you all,
only a few fragments of a disfigured life,
night walks through the desolation have taught me
the passion to prepare for a great dream:
down an old much travelled darkening road
near a river that reminds me of the Colorado,

I carry across my shoulders a shining elephant tusk.
I'm alone except for a dog, smart and alert,
that walks by my side and lightly leans against me
when I sit down to rest.

FALLING DOG

MICHAEL MOOS

I am lying on a giant dead sequoia.
I hear something at the top of the cliff,
among the stinging nettles and the madrona.
I open my eyes and see the sand wall
cave in, see the swallows' nests and lovers' names
disappear. A dog, a strong dark mongrel,
falls fifty feet through the air, his body
bouncing off this ancient tree with a thud.
I watch him, a moment, motionless on the sand.
I place my hand on his still rib cage.
His chest begins to rise and fall.
He stands, shakes once, hard, all over,
runs down the beach as if nothing had happened.
In one animal motion he shrugged off the pain . . .
No, the numbness from being uprooted . . .
What has taken me seventeen years,
an inch or so measured in this dead tree's rings.

THE THROES

DONALD MORRILL

In the photograph in the magazine, forty-eight lumberjacks and two
boys stand on the outer rings of a tree stump as large as a dance
floor, all but one wearing hats, following orders.

It is 1891 in 1991, the felling of the Mark Twain, Kings County,
California, in his hand now at a nameless pond in Virginia.

He rolls up the years, tight, and for distraction turns to water striders
on the surface of clouds a little darker as reflections.

A thousand miles away, his grandmother's body is going into the ground
with now flowers sent there as his emissary. Days before, he held
her, failing, goodbye.

He remembers her fists resting on her hips as her head rocked on the
cackle that silenced hotel lobbies; and she, an ancient widow, once
climbed onto a camel at the state fair, fascinated by the beast's green
tongue. He remembers the rusted well pump in her stories of childhood
on the hard, good farm.

"Nobody spoiled me," she said, nearing the end, "I spoiled myself."
And to her children all retired, "If you have questions about the
past, you best ask now."

He imagines lumberjacks restless for the paywagon, floozies shipped in
and mail-order brides—the gold rushing to a nearby town.

He thinks of the Twain (a seedling at the fall of Rome, unscarred by
fire or lightning, though of poor commercial quality). He envisions
the dynamited trunk lying outside the picture, and two giant slices of
it bound to London and New York, displayed there still, though
slightly shrunken.

Wondering about old measurements, he tries to count the striders before him; the combined, brief life; the pond his nameless feeling of the moment.

From out of the woods, a golden retriever appears, "Amy" according to her tag—in her jaws a three-foot length of branch she pushes into his hand, making him look at her.

He stands, hurls the limb into the water, Amy plunging after it— snorting, wrestling, returning it majestically over and over until he suddenly remembers the day the old woman taught him to throw . . .

He throws again, then, splashed by whatever tears the pond contains. The watery rings expand the magazine's circle of paper men. In their midst are crossed saws, five axes and twelve wedges upright like headstones.

WHAT THE DOG PERHAPS HEARS

LISEL MUELLER

If an audible whistle
blown between our lips
can send him home to us,
then silence is perhaps
the sound of spiders breathing
and roots mining the earth;
it may be asparagus heaving,
headfirst, into the light
and the long brown sound
of cracked cups, when it happens.
We would like to ask the dog
if there is a continuous whir
because the child in the house
keeps growing, if the snake
really stretches full length
without a click and the sun
breaks through the clouds without
a decibel of effort;
whether in autumn, when the trees
dry up their wells, there isn't a shudder
too high for us to hear.

What is it like up there
above the shut-off level
of our simple ears?
For us there was no birth-cry,
the newborn bird is suddenly here,
the egg broken, the nest alive,
and we heard nothing when the world changed.

The Black Dog: On Being a Poet

Joan Murray

So that coming to the low wall near the foreman's house
where a mare is nosing a stallion's heels, I might turn
and see a black dog walking up the hill—
ashamed that he was dozing and missed a scent,
and now it's filtered in and stirred him, and he must again
make that long, slow climb on stiff, unready joints,
pausing now and then to bark his warning,
yet all the time, his wagging tail.
Till I stand face to face with him: the pair of us
wondering what he'll do. He sniffs me liberally, then snorts
and shoves his head into the space he knows must be
beneath my hand, where it fits exactly and
lets me feel the old, intelligent skull.

And I think how long his journey's been—
How long that head evolved so that it fits my hand
while keeping all the scents of the world in order.
And how long my hand has been readying itself
to articulate around the sense of him. And how easily
that unsuspected part (once called the soul or heart) can
pass unnoticed through its unpatrolled borders and trespass
over into his. So that even after Sartre, even after Skinner,
we both can sense some purpose and volition as I stroke
with his ingenuous permission, the black dog's head.
Not to tame him. Not to elevate him. Or to use him only
as a prop for my cleverness. Not even to contain him
for a moment. But to let him move as he pleases—
even if it's back down the hill where he came from.
To move with him as he moves. To move
as he does. Till a door closes. Or opens.

ARF

JACK MYERS

Dogs give commands to me in one syllable,
the same one again and again.
I speak back in polysyllabics
above my one great bark.

It's like my dreams falling all night
in technicolor splendor. I can't remember what.
When I open my eyes and look back
I'm just grateful I fit my body through
this space as big as a bark.

And the conversations I have with myself each day. . . .
They're like those silver balls on poles
across which gags of burnt electricity arc.
And I'm laid out below, inert,
until my head smokes and I stagger off
with a grunt-thought, cough-out, my smashed send-off.

The same thing happened to my friend Larry
who claims he never woke up at birth.
So for $45 the holistic doctor placed a
bouillon cube on his forehead and a lump
of cheese over his heart, and Larry woke up
and coughed and coughed in dog language
and we knew to bring him water. It was a miracle!
Only we're not sure what.

I imagine that's why we have the public flasher
who is able to prepare us
for the right moment on some random day
when he'll drop the blinding light of his body

down in front of us: "Bark!"
He makes us feel exact.

My intuition tells me yes
even a stone can bark.
Only the sound it makes is millions of years long
and I'm standing in the silence and dark
between its two great phonemes of need,
going to sleep, waking up, going to sleep.

WALKING THE DOG

HOWARD NEMEROV

Two universes mosey down the street
Connected by love and a leash and nothing else.
Mostly I look at lamplight through the leaves
While he mooches along with tail up and snout down,
Getting a secret knowledge through the nose
Almost entirely hidden from my sight.

We stand while he's enraptured by a bush
Till I can't stand our standing any more
And haul him off; for our relationship
Is patience balancing to this side tug
And that side drag; a pair of symbionts
Contented not to think each other's thoughts.

What else we have in common's what he taught,
Our interest in shit. We know its every state
From steaming fresh through stink to nature's way
Of sluicing it downstreet dissolved in rain
Or drying it to dust that blows away.
We move along the street inspecting it.

His sense of it is keener far than mine,
And only when he finds the place precise
He signifies by sniffing urgently
And circles thrice about, and squats, and shits,
Whereon we both with dignity walk home
And just to show who's master I write the poem.

THE DOGS OF CHINLE

GREG PAPE

Once, camped at the mouth of the canyon,
I built a fire as the sun went down.
Horses grazed along the ridge, black
silhouettes on a deepening blue. A slight
breeze from the canyon moved the cottonwood
leaves. A smokey white dog drifted
under the trees, stopping now and then to read
whatever was written in scent on the air, to listen
into the distance to the dogs of Chinle.
I thought of a peace like this one broken
by Narbona's soldiers. It must have been
the dogs who first sensed their approach,
although the people knew they were coming.
A hundred women, children, and old men
hid in a cave high up in the canyon.
Canyon del Muerto. Massacre Cave.

Afterwards Narbona wrote to Chacon,
January 24, 1805 "The Corporal Balthasar
is bringing eighty-four pairs of ears
of as many Warriors and the six that are lacking
to complete the ninety which I report to your Lordship
were lost by the man in charge of them."
Because the human ear, by itself, is sexless
and because it is a funnel for lies
it is necessary to keep these records.

Now the horses loiter and graze openly
on the lawn of the high school, under
the cottonwoods, along the line of Russian olives,
and on the small patch of grass and dandelions
in front of the Department of Human Resources.

the dogs of Chinle must envy the horses
their stature and their station. Around
the town the horses move with a certain
dignity. When they step into the road cars
and pickups slow or stop to let them pass.
Whereas it seems the dogs are free game
on the streets of Chinle, and they know it.
They can smell it in the fur of the three-
legged ones, in the night breeze that blows
out of the canyon, in the morning air stilled
in the weeds along roadsides and ditches.

WHY PETS RUN THE WORLD

ROBERT PARHAM

Not much to say about collies
of course
or terriers
spending money that isn't theirs

but bulls
and danes
now there's a story to unfold

I've had
daydreams
about running over poodles
large or small

despite a youth of mongrel
at the foot
of the bed
to move me over into growth

sure! I've wondered why that spark
as if
from a gun
that would chase the only beasts

from the park
that is repose
all pet
all schmaltz

all there is is to be spared

Pavlov's Dog

Michael Pettit

Last night, late, a light rain
beading the windshield,
I held you and we listened
to the static and old songs on the radio.
Filled with the past, the failure
of love to last, beyond our breath
on the glass I saw coming
down the wet street a great dog,
his chestnut coat long and curling,
soaked as though he'd walked all night
to stand there before us.
I held you close and watched him
shut his yellow eyes
and shake slowly his massive head,
water slinging from his muzzle
in threads of light.
I watched him drive the muscles
of his neck and shoulders,
his back, flanks, hips a blur
of motion and water flowering.

And so I believed
love and sorrow must be foreign
to each other, the heart so large
they never meet, never speak.
Why is it not so? Why the old song,
desire and heartbreak we can sing
word for word after all these years?
Why as I held you did that dog
appear and seem to shake clean,
only to roll his eyes open
and stand unmoving, staring our way

through the rain? Cold and steady
and long into the night it fell,
into his thick coat, into my heart
where you walk, filled with love
and unafraid. I am afraid. Of Pavlov,
of his bell and saliva at work
in my life. Tell me how I am
to join you, to shake free for good
of that cold man's rain,
his dog standing wet, obedient,
and brutal as a bell ringing,
always ringing, for sorrow.

'COON DOGS

MICHAEL PFEIFER

for Uncle Sterling, Mark, and my father

RED BONE

Still hound
light
the patience of dirt
the third of the world
between sky and water
shoulder and stone skull
hunched under the sky
appealing to it
like red chert
hackles lifting like dust

BLUETICK

Energetic
mysterious voice at evening
like swallows
coming from the open barn door
from everywhere
a carbide lantern
hissing far off
or the trickle of water
through limestone
white as the moon

BLACK AND TAN

Night hound
that cannot retreat
but carries something
soft and bitter
gurgles
in the throat

like whiskey
the others follow this one
into death
its secret home.

PANEGYRIC FOR GEE

STANLEY PLUMLY

The anachronistic face of the bulldog,
the anachronistic, Churchillian face of the bulldog,
the anachronistic, Churchillian, gargoylean
face of the bulldog, the anachronistic, Churchillian,
gargoylean, Quasimodian face of the bulldog,
whose ears are silk purses,
whose eyes, like a bullfrog's, enlarge,
whose flat black wet gorilla's nose sucks the air
out of the dust, whose mouth is as wide
as a channel cat's feeding for years in solitude
on the bottom, whose two lower utter canines
show one at a time, bite that is worse than its bark,
whose slobber is the drool of herbivores,
whose brooding pose is the seal's,
who climbs and descends, who stands, who climbs again,
who at the top of the stairs in the morning dark
is beef-faced drowsy as the mastiff god—
the andiron-large front legs welded like doorstops to the paws—
who peers down from prehistory over the edge.
O gnomic skin and bone too big for a soul
squeezed from a root-slip in the earth,
O antediluvian noises in the throat,
O silences of staring straight ahead,
O dogtrot, O dreams of the chase ten yards and then a rest—.
To sleep by a bulldog is to return to the primal nasal
sleep of the drunk, the drunk whose carnal snore self-purifies
the breath with the sanctity of opera,
the rich deep long great breath of the animal breached but flying.
When my father slept he slept the sleep of a drunk

who'd have loved this bulldog, so stubborn at the forehead,
so set on plowing through to the conclusion of a door
too thick to pass, except in spirit,
whose singing sober voice alone breaks hearts.

BAD DOG

LAWRENCE RAAB

"Just remember," my friend told me,
"you can't take it personally."
We were talking about the new dog
who ate things—a book one night, then
a pair of glasses—who clawed at the screens
when we were gone. How much remorse
would be sufficient? She lay down
on her back, legs up, eyes
averted. She gave herself over
to whatever cruelties we couldn't
manage to inflict, who were wondering
what it would mean, hours later, to brandish
the shredded piece of evidence and proclaim
the single, necessary word—
"No, no!" we insisted, and of course
she cast her eyes to the wall
and the way she trembled beneath us
looked like compliance, and then
almost like understanding, almost like
those bargains we make
every day when we talk to each other.

To a Collie Pup

Carl Rakosi

Nobody had to show you
where the sun is
or that my back
could serve the same purpose
as a tree.

Why, you are hardly old enough
to know the difference
between your tail and a shadow,
yet the warm radiator
and your bowl of water
are already old friends.

The way you look up at me
with a saint in each eye
one would never suspect
that you chase birds and chickens
and steal stale bread
from the neighbor's trashcan.

Lay off, you beggar,
I just fed you
and took you walking.

Go spring
into the autumn leaves.
Nuzzle and roll
as if there were nothing
in the whole wide world
but fun.

How is it
that you play
with my shoelace
and understand so well
how to love me?

For this you shall have
the key to my bedroom
and the degree
of master of arts.

DEATH OF A DOG

BIN RAMKE

from Secrets of the Saints

The wearing of time on the wrist
reveals the modern soul: once
it was kept in a pocket
somewhere near the liver; some
still hang it from a chain
around the neck symbolically.

At Touro Infirmary the Mexicans
always pay cash. One couple
for three years paid every week
on the death of their child
born premature, killed by time
or its absence. In the modern mode
this is called a time-payment.

Whatever else hangs in the summer air
around those front steps ticks
silently but strong, like humidity
in New Orleans in June. I held
other jobs in that city, but none
that made me miss so much my dog
whose heart one day was not sufficient
unto the troubles thereof.

He loved me like clockwork while he lived.

DOG

DAVID RAY

The cosmos and all its mysteries so ample
do not concern him.
      Or perhaps they concern me too much!

He's not bothered by this or by that—
         my dog, who does not travel far,
no more than we walk or now and then drive.

Yet when I stood in New Zealand
and looked up at the Southern Cross,
      so famous, so appallingly
disappointing, he was the one I longed
      to speak to, share my regret with.
I knew he'd console me,

my little black dog they would not even let
into their country, whom they would assume
      the worst of, whom they distrust

without even seeing him or knowing
how fine and loving he is whom they scorn,
keeping even the expensive sight
      of their puny stars
         out of his amber eyes.

No wonder I left them "down under"—those people
who call themselves Kiwis—after a flightless bird—
      and returned to my little black dog

      to walk with him and to practice
the gentleness,
      quick forgiveness he taught me.

THE OLD DOG

DAVID RAY

The dog gazes at his food,
waiting for something better.
It's rubbed off on him,
this human fault,
      this fatal flaw,

this vice of waiting,
passing up what's offered.
He's watched and learned—
      all the wrong lessons,
and may well stand and starve.

The day's gold drops around him.
The scorned bowl glows.

THIS

ADRIENNE RICH

Face flashing free   child-arms
lifting the collie pup
torn paper on the path
Central Park   April '72
behind you   minimal
those benches and that shade
that brilliant light in which
you laughed longhaired
and I'm the keeper of
this little piece of paper
this little piece of truth

I wanted this from you—
laughter   a child turning
into a boy   at ease
in the spring light   with friends
I wanted this for you

I could mutter   *Give back*
that day   *give me again*
that child   *with the chance*
of making it all right
I could yell   *Give back that light*
on the dog's teeth   *the child's hair*
but no rough drafts are granted
—Do you think I don't remember?
did you think I was all-powerful?
unimpaired   unappalled?
yes   you needed that from me
I wanted this from you

POEM TO BEGIN THE SECOND DECADE OF AIDS

BOYER RICKEL

The dog, alive, Lucy, my light, sleeps
    on the couch I'd have trained her off of
had not someone coaxed her, repeatedly,
    to clamber up, then lie down along
his outstretched legs; Gary, alive, who,

    had he had his way at first, wouldn't
have let her live with us at all for fear
    she'd dig up the bulbs and seedlings,
or strip the bark from young acacias
    and mesquites in our yard alive with

four years of his ceaseless shovel, shoulder,
    rake and sweat. The hour darkens, sweetens,
whenever I ask how long for all this—
    November lettuces, April poppies, Lucy's
dog-fragrant, humid *hrumph* across my

    rising/falling, almost-sleeping chest,
how long the *chauk, chauk* of Gary's spade,
    the swells and waves of caliche and dust.
This poem is far too private for anybody
    but us. This poem will make certain

close friends blush, who prefer poems be
    like linens they can put in drawers,
sure of their place and use. Today I
    thought of this as I took up our blue
wool blanket, a week-long winter freeze

having passed, folding once, twice,
a cloudless, geometrically diminishing sky;
        then twice again, all compact, tangible
potential, ready to unfold and warm or
        simply drape across a reclining form.

TRYING TO WRITE YOU A POEM
ON OUR ANNIVERSARY
WHILE DOWNSTAIRS
YOU ROUGHHOUSE WITH THE DOGS

MICHAEL J. ROSEN

With a vocabulary of imitations,
babytalk, and slang, you, dear, give voice
to everything: the door, linoleum,
a treat . . . gradually, the house itself
(at least its lower orders) assumes the secret
language of conspiracy—celebration,

rather, of simply coming inside, of simply
being companions who have conceded more
than a little boyishness, more than a little
doggishness, to the other unknowable side.
But save a word or two I *can* distinguish,
the roughhousing, the house itself, encodes

your exclamations (not unlike our own
affection's temporary and tidy shorthand)
in patterns of stops and starts, scraping nails,
whoops, dead silences, and barks
that might communicate for all you know.
I don't know. It's hard to ignore, harder

still to attend, yet sometimes I've discerned
news that's news to me in your doggerel
and doubletalk (for you must answer, too)
and voices that I recognize as yours
and yet you've never never used with me. Ah hah!
The key to the code is that it won't be cracked,

or calmed like poetry—what I hear,
conducted through wall vents, conveyed up the stairwell,
is how we always must sound to the dogs: tones
divorced from the particular, a *now*
followed by other *nows*, with nothing like
our proud and inconsistent details confusing

the issue—which is always trust, isn't it,
whether we betray it or not, call it
love or not, or any other word
(or words—or lack of words) to justify
the way we want to feel and behave and seem
to construe a world given to disaffection?

Now: laughter leaps two stairs at a time,
an unmistakable word "Michael" that means
"Let's go see Michael." Ahead by a nose,
the dogs skid into the room and nudge my hands
from their devotion, whether ot not they see it
as that, or understand the broken silence.

ELEGY FOR A BEAGLE MUTT

LIZ ROSENBERG

What a season this is:
darkness making its sure descent, the motley rose
of drooping head, and wet leaves plastered everywhere
in bright chaotic paths. My leaping pup—
she of the quick pulse coiled
on the bed who slept in outlandish,
graceful twists of the neck,
shook by the door, lay dripping on the porch,
broke the spines of rabbits and squirrels,
begged at every table, that last morning
rose from the foot of the bed
thrusting her jaw into my face to stare:
stern, puzzled, forgiving glance, crushed
under a school bus, gone.
The sprawl of bones with pomp and grief
is laid to rest beneath a rusty tree—
and still I see her low shape moving
cautiously through every raining bush
or flashing under weeds as flaps of newspaper blow by.
If I had been out walking,
if I had thrown myself into her childish play,
she who skittered and obeyed could have led me,
licking the hand of every passing soul, and pulled me
willy-nilly through the final gate. Now the corpse commands
and I stay here, reminded of the Buddhist saint
who waited at the gates of heaven
ten thousand years with his faithful dog, till both
were permitted in. Lithe dancer, I am reeling on a planet
gone to dark moods and imbalance, silent and unsafe,
imagining your collar of bones hooked small
under my fist—wait for me!

SUSQUEHANNA

LIZ ROSENBERG

Those many dark nights in our wedding house.
Hundreds of them—like fireflies—
above the quiet road till dawn,
and still I can't remember even
one of the naked trips he made downstairs
to bring me back a glass of water:
agéd, sagging, fly-footed one.
Then the dog would sneak into our room
and groan and settle his bones down
on the wood floor, heavily.

I knew we were all going to die
but not then, and not right away;
because in those days
there were more days to come.
I thought I could not
run out of them.

THE THREE-LEGGED DOG

DENNIS SCHMITZ

which I wanted as allegory,
pushes his snout, all hair-commas & snot,

against my pants-leg.
The party's host coaxes in dog-patois, coaxes

both of us back from revulsion,
from Art. Up close, I see the actual

harness steadying some leg
device, studs & leather-wound wood piece—

the dog wobbles
but moves. Neither of us is enticed

by sauce-painted
shrimps or the party canapés, but by despair,

a state so low man goes in
on all fours, either as dog,

which prefers flesh,
or the ingenuous lamb which eats

its own mood.
The dog holds up his snout, & I look

in the loose-lipped cleft
at teeth, phlegmatic, the only one of his retinue

attentive.

My Dog and I Grow Fat

James Seay

His true grace, the dog books hold,
Is witnessed only in the field,
And I suppose our yard's
A field of sorts—
His Irish eye is smiling on the sparrow there,
He stalks the squirrel as a king's dog would exotic birds,
And springs like bright wire
After butterflies,
Wildly outside his droll household self.
He takes their minor flights as threats against
His bones, yet is able only to wolf
An occasional loose feather or taste of butterfly dust.

My crew-cut neighbor hints
It's a shame he's not been trained to hunt,
Says it'd lean him down
And he wouldn't grow dull.
He's gun shy, I say, can't hold a point.
Our talk dwindles to the time he's having with his crew-cut lawn,
The drought.
We ease away, I to these poems,
My dog to our riot of weeds.
When the neighbor is inside
I write a poem wherein my dog
And I grow fat on butterfly dust.

Tonight we chase the lightning bugs
To work off fat and keep from growing dull.

LIVING SNOW

BRENDA SHAW

The gulls arrive in a white cloud
and spiral to a stop on Magdalene Green.
They settle in little separate flakes,
cover the grass.
Here and there an eddy, a local flurry—
but the main mass is still,
safe from the gale at sea.

The black and white mongrel
likes snow.
With lunges of delight
she sends it swirling
back into the sky.

COUNTRY FAIR

CHARLES SIMIC

If you didn't see the six-legged dog,
It doesn't matter.
We did, and he mostly lay in the corner.
As for the extra legs,

One got used to them quickly
And thought of other things.
Like, what a cold, dark night
To be out at the fair.

Then the keeper threw a stick
And the dog went after it
On four legs, the other two flapping behind,
Which made one girl shriek with laughter.

She was drunk and so was the man
Who kept kissing her neck.
The dog got the stick and looked back at us.
And that was the whole show.

MADDY'S WOODS

JIM SIMMERMAN

That crusty, good man John Fife
pretended to blow his nose. . . .
In just one night her breathing

had grown labored, raspy
as a punctured squeeze-box;
her mouth cold, a pocket of ice.

I pretended, earlier, in the dark
back room, to follow the concise
lesson in black and white

textbook photos, in shadowy
x rays, back-lit, pinned to the wall
like the pelts of ghosts:

how the normal canine heart
is ovoid, a fist-sized egg
in the nest of the ribs;

and how this one's heart
had enlarged, swelled up
like an over-inflated balloon. . . .

By now she could hardly walk.
By now she was wrapped
in a blanket on the floor,

and when she raised her head
once, to look around the room,
her eyes saw what?—

we might have been mist;
we might have been aspens
rooted in snow. It's time

to go walking in Maddy's woods,
where a hawk throws a shadow
you could chase through the trees,

where the tough, thorny branch
of a wild rose clings
to a little scrap of fur,

and all those smells
on the breath of the wind
make you crazy in the nose.

It's time to go
down on all fours and dig
deep into the frozen bed of the woods,

and let the heart rest
that ran so hard, that grew
too big for this world.

FETCH

JIM SIMMERMAN

The marrow it's this:
that night after night I dream
you alive, dream you clawing
up and through the snarl
of spade-lopped roots and loam,
through the cairn beneath the pine
in a bower of pines, a wildwood
of pines, beneath a wheeling moon—
shaking from your body
the tattered blanket, shaking
from your throat the collar
of blood—the ball
in your mouth where I left it,
your coat wet where I kissed it—
breaking through underbrush
onto the trail, tracking it back
to the tire-rutted road—
loping now, running now—
your nostrils flared
and full of the world—
ignoring the squirrel,
ignoring the jay, ignoring
the freeway's litter of bones—
night nearly dead as you
bolt for the lane,
up the drive, into the yard—
panting now, breathing now—
racing from door to window to door,
scratching at the screen,
whining at the glass, the ball
in your mouth—Lo,
wouldn't I shake from this

sweet gnawed dream to rise
and fetch you in
with the light that returns
me day after day,
takes you again and again.

Leo by Charles Rue Woods

BARK WITH AUTHORITY

MAURYA SIMON

I tell my dog, bête noire of the backyard,
unbellicose beast, he with the musculature
of a canine warrior, all beef and brawn;
bark with Byzantine glory, with bravura,
bark with the rumblings of ruptured nerve:
be brazen and boisterous, be jowled in howls,
be loose in the lungs, a grounded leviathan;
be blue in the throat from sounding an alarm.
Rip your voice through the dazzle of the rich,
through the daze of the poor, through storm
and drought, through the whines of Boy Scouts
out on their hike, through coyote's whistle;
rouse your ruff to a roar that ripples
the air like a serrated knife, that riots
in the ear until the world shouts Stop!
But you, sad Sam, named for the word-man
who barked out a lexicon of rapturous sounds,
you with your doleful eyes, crooked smile,
with your quizzical gaze, your velvet snout:
you shrug your shoulders, tune me out,
would rather stand shyly behind old Molly,
your surrogate dam, that grizzled old bitch,
arthritic and wobbly, though still wily—
you'd rather demur to her dominance, yes?
Well, what's it to me if you'd prefer modesty,
being the foil, the sidekick, Laurel to Hardy?
What do I care if you live out your days,
indeed your dog days, without doggerel or dog-
eared memories, with a dogged suspicion, dog-
faced and dog-headed and -hearted, that you've
gone, dog-gone it, to the dogs, so to speak,

and that your only dogma, your only dog's letter
(trilled in your sleep when you're dog-tired)
that weathers your lips begins with an "S"—
and ushers in snoozing and supper and silence?

How It Began

William Stafford

They struggled their legs and blindly loved, those puppies
inside my jacket as I walked through town. They crawled
for warmth and licked each other—their poor mother
dead, and one kind boy to save them. I spread
my arms over their world and hurried along.

At Ellen's place I knocked and waited—the tumult
invading my sleeves, all my jacket alive.
When she came to the door we tumbled—black, white
gray, hungry—all over the living room floor
together, rolling, whining, happy, and blind.

DEAR MARVIN,

WILLIAM STAFFORD

I merge with your message "Wherever
You Are." I learn what it is like to
have soft ears that compose whatever comes
into a symphony, to hear as a silver
sound the whole imminent world.
You wake up my instinct for puppyhood
and bring that summer bubble around me:
forgiveness everywhere, a yearning, a grace
coming out of awkwardness to capture
us, a touch from the beginning of things.

These beings that call each other "Prince"
or "Queenie" or "Duke," they can fetch
history along with reminders, nothing
ever quite ending—even a rose
twining out a tapering faintness toward other
seasons; and all things coming are announced
by a computer chip of sense that embodies
where they are from and how long on the way.

For awhile, reading your lines, I ran
on your trail so well I could never be lost.
And sometimes when you turned I was already
there, your very best friend.

—Bill.

THE WOLVES

FRANK STANFORD

at night while the dogs
were barking
Baby Gauge and I crawled under the fence
with knives
we made out like the rattlesnake melons
were men we didn't like
the new moon ones were wolves
I would cut a belly this way
he would cut a belly that way
the flies
came around the sweet juice
it was blood to us
we tasted it we licked it off the blades
we decided not to kill the wolves
we wanted to be wolves
we stuck the knives in the ground
the moon shined on them
we turned the pilot caps inside out
so the fur would show
that way when we crawled
under the bob wire
a little piece would get caught
we wouldn't though
we wanted to leave trails
but no scents
we tore the melons open we licked the blood off our paws
we wanted to be wolves
and in the morning all those dead men
with their hearts eat out

LOVE FOR THE DOG

GERALD STERN

Before he opened his eyes, as he lay there under the window,
he was convinced he would be able to speak this time and sort things
    out
clearly as he did when his tongue was still a hammer;
a half hour later he was once again on the chair
with all these keepers staring at him in pity and fear
and giving him milk and cocoa and white napkins.
In the middle of his exhausted brain there rose a metaphor
of an animal, a dog, with a broken spine, sliding around
helplessly in the center of the slippery floor
with loving owners all around encouraging him
and the dog trying desperately to please them.
He sat there proud of his metaphor, tears of mercy in his eyes,
unable in his dumbness to explain his pleasure,
unable now even to rise because of the spine.
He felt only love for the dog,
all different from the ugly muscular cat
which had leaped the day before on his bony thigh
as if it were a tree limb or an empty chair,
as if he could not run again if he had to,
as if there was not life still pouring out voluptuously
like wild water through all his troubled veins.

THE DOG

GERALD STERN

What was I doing with my white teeth exposed
like that on the side of the road I don't know,
and I don't know why I lay beside the sewer
so that the lover of dead things could come back
with his pencil sharpened and his piece of white paper.
I was there for a good two hours whistling
dirges, shrieking a little, terrifying
hearts with my whimpering cries before I died
by pulling the one leg up and stiffening.
There is a look we have with the hair of the chin
curled in mid-air, there is a look with the belly
stopped in the midst of its greed. The lover of dead things
stoops to feel me, his hand is shaking. I know
his mouth is open and his glasses are slipping.
I think his pencil must be jerking and the terror
of smell—and sight—is overtaking him;
I know he has that terrified faraway look
that death brings—he is contemplating. I want him
to touch my forehead once and rub my muzzle
before he lifts me up and throws me into
that little valley. I hope he doesn't use
his shoe for fear of touching me; I know,
or used to know, the grasses down there; I think
I knew a hundred smells. I hope the dog's way
doesn't overtake him, one quick push,
barely that, and the mind freed, something else,
some other thing, to take its place. Great heart,
great human heart, keep loving me as you lift me,
give me your tears, great loving stranger, remember
the death of dogs, forgive the yapping, forgive
the shitting, let there be pity, give me your pity.
How could there be enough? I have given

my life for this, emotion has ruined me, oh lover,
I have exchanged my wildness—little tricks
with the mouth and feet, with the tail, my tongue is a parrot's,
I am a rampant horse, I am a lion,
I wait for the cookie, I snap my teeth—
as you have taught me, oh distant and brilliant and lonely.

THE BLACK MOTH

FRANK STEWART

Large as a hand, the black mosaic moth
comes out in the early morning.
I am alone on the steps of the cabin
with the silent forest.
Unlike the paired white butterflies
that rise in helix flight,
the moth stumbles into the low branches
of the young Israeli apple to hide. I know
when I have hurt you it was not from weakness
but from too much hunger. The rain in turn
hurts me now, and the dogs with their love
and the faithfulness which they cannot help.

DOGS, HER DREAMING

PAMELA STEWART

for Sheba and Sue

The *always* of it is that she falls
into the red-eyed dark: from a plane
twisting down through fire to the sea, or
that truck smashing her spine
into the wall between church and street.
This blank, black *always* of her dream
condenses her to ember and bone until,
suddenly, she spirits onto a forest path.
Arms swinging, she strides
to a clearing full of dogs and their noise.
All the dogs of her life—from crib
to kitchen, hospital to garden—
rush to greet and surround her
with delighted tails, jowls, paws and tongue.

So, having just stuffed four mailboxes at the top of the hill full
of cards, bills, catalogues and this week's *Town Crier*, she shoves
her beat-to-shit blue Honda into 4th, speeds down the mud-
frozen slope till one deep rut catches, tips and throws her falling.
The car on its back like a spider in from the rain. Her satchel,
and the U.S. Mail sliding out the window onto ice. On stomach
and elbows she slides too, rises in return from spinning into the bright
winter's noon. Hands, jaw, legs shaking, she turns
to limp that downhill mile to the next house, starts and sees
one dog waiting at forest's edge. A small Husky
with milky eyes fits itself right against her slow-
lifting knee, holds warm and hard to her side all the way down.

Learning at the post office counter,
this is what she said—how the dream
never exhausts itself. I nod,
happy to believe. Now

on the windowglass beside my chair,
is the smallest, fastest spider I've ever seen.
I lean close, peer into a tiny white glow
where its heart might be
until it vanishes in a crevice of the sill.
What a vast, exacting world
I've yet to learn from creatures of this earth:
their tongues, teeth, wings, ears and paws—
what they know of rising from the red-eyed dark.

NEWFOUNDLAND-PRAISE

PAMELA STEWART

On days I don't feel pretty I go downstairs
and watch my dog stretch and yawn awake.
Molly doesn't care how my lank, electric hair
sticks to my mouth, how my eyelids swell
from bad dreams. Molly's happy as I reach
for kibble and bowl. She leaps, paws wide
and slick as saucers on the wooden floor.

Molly's curious, craves apple peels, grapes
and moist California prunes which go like glue
against her tongue. She twists and gums
like someone who hasn't put her teeth in yet.
When I shower, Molly thrusts in her head, licks
my knees of soap and lies right across the doorway
so no one we don't know can sneak in from the woods.

Molly loves it when I curl up to read. Her nose,
wild and black as a train, plunges the pages
on my lap. *Wahroof-woof-wrooo = Let me out
to play* with ball, stick, or face full of mud.
She brings it all to show me, shakes out
her coat of grit and leaves, sighing down
with belly up, she goes to sleep and snores.

Molly doesn't care about make-up (except to taste)
or what I wear, prefers to trot-trot down the drive
for mail, proudly bearing papers home
in drool-shined teeth. Tail pluming, she
sashays to her bed and grins beneath dark
sexy lashes. *Aren't I good?*
Molly knows which hand finds the biscuit box.

Sometimes she howls at moonshine, or a rustle
in the trees. She's scared of light
on midnight shapes. Molly's absolute and clear.
She pulls my own love out against the air
as her huge body presses toward me.
Molly undoes my vanities and fear so I
feel almost safe.

UNCLE DOG: THE POET AT 9

ROBERT SWARD

I did not want to be old Mr.
Garbage man, but uncle dog
Who rode sitting beside him.

Uncle dog had always looked
To me to be a truck-strong
Wise-eyed, a cur-like Ford

Of a dog. I did not want
To be Mr. Garbage man because
All he had was cans to do.

Uncle dog sat there me-beside-him
Emptying nothing. Barely even
Looking from garbage side to side:

Like rich people in the backseats
Of chauffeur-cars, only shaggy
In an unwagging tall-scrawny way.

Uncle dog belonged any just where
He sat, but old Mr. Garbage man
Had to stop at everysingle can.

I thought. I did not want to be Mr.
Everybody calls them that first.
A dog is said, Dog! Or by name.

I would rather be called Rover
Than Mr. And sit like a tough
Smart mongrel beside a garbage man.

Uncle dog always went to places
Unconcerned, without no hurry.
Independent like some leashless

Toot. Honorable among scavenger
Can-picking dogs. And with a bitch
At every other can. And meat:

His for the barking. Oh, I wanted
To be uncle dog—sharp, high fox-
Eared, cur-Ford truck-faced

With his pick of the bones.
A doing, truckman's dog
And not a simple child-dog

Nor friend to man, but an uncle
Traveling, and to himself—
And a bitch at every second can.

CLANCY THE DOG

ROBERT SWARD

for Claire

He is so ugly he is a psalm to ugliness,
this extraterrestrial, shorthaired
midget sea lion,
snorts, farts, grunts, turns somersaults
on his mistress's bed.

She calls him an imperfect Boston terrier,
part gnome, part elf,
half something and half something else,
180,000,000-year-old Clancy
with his yellowy-white, pin-pointy teeth
and red, misshapen prehistoric gums.

Clancy has no tail at all and doesn't bark.
He squeaks like a monkey,
flies through the air,
lands at six every morning
on his mistress's head,
begging to be fed and wrapped not in a robe
but a spread.

Tree frog, warthog, groundhog,
"Clancy, Clancy," she calls for him
in the early morning fog,
and he appears, anything, anything,
part anything but a dog.

DOG

SUNTARO TANIKAWA

Trans. Harold Wright

Sadder than myself
there is a dog
there—
down the alley
silent
cowering
only his eyes are wide open
nobody calls him
nobody notices him
when I am sad
sadder than myself,
there is a dog
always
there
beside me
never begging for pity,
merely
there.

AUGUST AND FEBRUARY

SUNTARO TANIKAWA

Trans. Harold Wright

The boy put the puppy in a basket.
The boy put the puppy in a basket
                    and weighted it down.
The boy was crying.
The cicadas were very noisy.

      The girl's room was cold;
      we were covered with many blankets.
      The girl's body smelled of dry grass.
      At dusk   sleet was falling.

The boy looked at the basket
                    there on the river bank.
The puppy wagged its tail.
The sun was nearly scorching.

      In the dimness of the room
      we were soaked with sweat;
      then finally soundly went to sleep.

The boy shutting his eyes
                  threw the basket into the river,
and then still crying he ran away.

      When we opened our eyes
      it was already dark outside.

The boy that night couldn't stop crying.

PEARL AND I ARE FAR TOO FAT

ELIZABETH MARSHALL THOMAS

My granddaughters named her Pearl, not me.
I name dogs for sky things, wild things, weather.
Suessi (wolf in Finnish),
Windigo, Sundog and Chinook.
Those were my dogs.

Still, Pearl suits her.
An Aussie shepherd, she has lustre.
She's also beyond price.
And if this Pearl were cast
before a swine,
he'd soon become a swine before a Pearl
to pigtrot where she drove him.

Once Pearl and I were thin.
Back then
we'd climb our narrow staircase side by side
and on a narrow bed we'd sleep entwined

But now we're wide.
Asleep we need more space,
and feeling crowded, shove each other.
I bow my back against her feet,
she works me to the edge.
I wake and cry, Oh Pearl, move over.

Obliging even in her sleep, she shifts her bulk a little.

No longer do we use the staircase side by side.
Once, going down, I made her wait while I,

hand on the bannister, foot poised to step,
began without her.

We're off, she thought, and rushed right by.

Straight to the floor below I plunged
and mildly injured, wept.

Helpfully, she covered me with kisses.

DOG'S DEATH

JOHN UPDIKE

She must have been kicked unseen or brushed by a car.
Too young to know much, she was beginning to learn
To use the newspapers spread on the kitchen floor
And to win, wetting there, the words, "Good dog! Good dog!"

We thought her shy malaise was a shot reaction.
The autopsy disclosed a rupture in her liver.
As we teased her with play, blood was filling her skin
And her heart was learning to lie down forever.

Monday morning, as the children were noisily fed
And sent to school, she crawled beneath the youngest's bed.
We found her twisted limp but still alive.
In the car to the vet's, on my lap, she tried

To bite my hand and died. I stroked her warm fur
And my wife called in a voice imperious with tears.
Though surrounded by love that would have upheld her,
Nevertheless she sank and, stiffening, disappeared.

Back home, we found that in the night her frame,
Drawing near to dissolution, had endured the shame
Of diarrhoea and had dragged across the floor
To a newspaper carelessly left there. *Good dog.*

DIVINE RIGHT

GLORIA VANDO

*Do you believe in Chairman Mao and refuse
to curb your dog?*
from Yvonne Rainer's film Christine

Mao says sit.
Mao says beg.
Mao never asks
how d'ya wanna see Hitler?
Mao says roll over,
play dead—and means it.
Mao floats down the Yangtze
bellyup
without waterwings.
Mao is Chairman
of the bored.

My great dane Napoleon
eats when he chooses, sits
when he wants to,
his tail splits
infinitives
with a scythelike swing
we do not question.
He doesn't know
of Chairmen or Führers,
doesn't give a shit
about political alternatives.
He's King.

NIGHTSHADE

ELLEN BRYANT VOIGT

The dog lay under the house, having crawled
back beyond the porch, bellying
beneath the joists through rocks and red dirt
to the cool stone foundation where it died
as the children called and sobbed;
and now their father had to wrench it out,
the one he had been breaking to handle birds.

This was a man of strictest moderation,
who had heard a dash of strychnine in its meat
could be a tonic for a dog, an extra edge.
He loved that dog, and got the dosage wrong.
And I loved my father—
I was among the children looking on—
and for years would not forgive him:

without pure evil in this world,
there was no east or west, no polestar
and no ratifying dove. I sat inside
the small white house for hours,
deaf to the world, playing my two songs,
one in a major, the other in a sad, minor key.

THE TRUST

ELLEN BRYANT VOIGT

Something was killing sheep
but it was sheep this dog attended on the farm—
a black-and-white border collie, patrolling his fold
like a parish priest. The second time the neighbor came,
claiming to have spotted the dog at night, a crouched figure
slithering toward the pen on the far side of the county,
the farmer let him witness how the dog,
alert and steady, mended the frayed
edge of the flock, the clumped sheep calm
as they drifted together along the stony hill.
But still more sheep across the glen were slaughtered,
and the man returned more confident. This time,
the master called his dog forward,
and stroking the eager head, prized open the mouth to find,
wound around the base of the back teeth—squat molars
the paws can't reach to clean—small coils of wool,
fine and stiff, like threads from his own jacket.
So he took down the rifle from the rack
and shot the dog and buried him,
his best companion in the field for seven years.
Once satisfied, the appetite is never dulled again.
Night after night, its sweet insistent promise
drives the animal under the rail fence and miles away
for a fresh kill; and with guilty cunning brings him back
to his familiar charges, just now stirring in the early light,
brings him home to his proud husbandry.

OLD DOG

NANCY B. WALL

When her rabies tag arrived in the mail
I tossed it on the kitchen counter.
She won't jump the wall
Or jerk the leash from my hand and bolt.

Years ago she disappeared on our morning walk
An elegant black streak on the first white-hot day of summer
Lured up a hill from the arroyo
By a deer, a rabbit, the irresistable, dizzying scent of freedom.
That night, certain the desert had claimed her
I struggled to let go
But at dawn, her coat matted, trailing cactus,
She rolled into the kitchen when I opened the door.
Grinning, she drained her water dish and collapsed on the tile
To sleep off her foolishness.

This morning she staggers to her feet, rear end listing oddly,
And hangs back, though we walk only to the end of the street.
She cannot see the rabbit dart directly in front of her
From its cover of rock and desert broom,
Does not respond to the repeated yelp
Of the alarm on the neighbor's car.

At home again, I pick up her tag and work the stiff metal ring apart
Forcing it onto her collar
As if a simple act of will, a talisman
Can hold back time.

DOGS IN THE STORM

MICHAEL WATERS

after Akhamatova

When this slow heart was raging
and I could tell no one, especially you,
I would abandon the exhaustion of sheets,
this woman tossing like damp leaves,

and storm a few miles into the country.
I wanted to memorize the silhouette
of each branch, the chorus of stars,
the uproar of the willows' shadows,

the stiff mailboxes bearing witness
to such immense drift and flux.
I wanted to not think about you.
But each time some stray bitch

came limping along the highway,
eyes iced shut in the wind, nose
scenting the hunger of wild couplings,
I wondered: Whose lost lover is this?

And how far away is my distant brother
who howls for us both in such savage moonlight?

VILLAGE DOGS

MICHAEL WATERS

Quantico, 1990

Groggy, we watched the ball descend
   as benediction upon the boisterous
      throng overflowing Times Square.
         We felt no desire

to mill there, to embrace the New
   Year among strangers, jostled and cold.
      Corks still popping at nearby
         parties, I leashed the dog only

minutes past midnight and let him lead me
   onto the village street, its one lamp
      a low moon lustrous below black
         clouds, glazed with rain.

What remained unspoken between us followed me
   like a shadow in a B movie, then sprang
      through a hedge-wall with a primal
         snarl. A pit bull, frothing

knot of muscle, slammed into my pet like a small
   train, tumbling him, his high-pitched
      yelps rising above their revved
         thrashings and the revelers' shouts.

I kicked and missed and thudded onto my back
   inches from their slathered, blood-
      slick snouts. *Match days of sorrow,*
         decrees Psalm 90, *with days of joy . . .*

I rose and dragged my broken dog
   by the choke-chain toward the house,

        the bull still clamped to his throat
            till I splintered a branch across its spine.

By now my wife stood pale on the porch
    as I hefted a brick to crush
        its skull, but her cry stopped my arm:
            "Don't. Haven't you done enough harm?"

The bull foamed in the hedge's shadow.
    I hurled the brick into its ribs
        and the creature—my stunted anger—
            fled with a groan. And when I returned

home, bruised and sober, the neighbors'
    festive clamor dwindling
        in the decade's first hour, who
            could deny that the marriage was over?

MAY

BRUCE WEIGL

I wanted to stay with my dog
when they did her in
I told the young veterinarian
who wasn't surprised.
Shivering on the chrome table,
she did not raise her eyes to me when I came in.
Something was resolved in her.
Some darkness exchanged for the pain.
There were a few more words
about the size of her tumor and her age,
and how we wanted to stop her suffering,
or our own, or stop all suffering
from happening before us
and then the nurse shaved May's skinny leg
with those black clippers;
she passed the needle to the doctor
and for once I knew what to do
and held her head against mine.
I cleaved to that smell
and lied into her ear
that it would be all right.
The veterinarian, whom I'd fought
about when to do this thing
said through tears
that it would only take a few minutes
as if that were not a long time
but there was no cry or growl,
only the weight of her in my arms,
and then on the world.

DOGS

BRUCE WEIGL

I bought a bar girl in Saigon
cigarettes, watches, and Tide soap
to sell on the black market
and she gave me a room to sleep in
and all the cocaine I could live through
those nights I had to leave.
I would sometimes meet them, on the stairs,
and she would be wrapped in the soldier
who was always drunk, smiling,
her smell all over him.

She ran once to the room screaming
about dogs and pulled me down to the street
where a crowd of Vietnamese gathered
watching two stuck.
The owners fought about whose fault it was.
The owner of the male took off his sandal,
began to beat the female;
the owner of the female
kicked the male
but they did not part,
the beating made her tighten
and her tightening made him swell
as she dragged him down the street
the crowd running after them.

I remembered my grandfather,
how his pit bull locked up
the same way with the neighbor's dog.
The neighbor screamed and kicked
and the cop with his nightstick
sucked his teeth and circled

the dogs as the dogs circled.
Yet my grandfather knew what to do—
not cold water, warm,
warm, and pour it slow.

DAY AFTER CHASING PORCUPINES

JAMES WELCH

Rain came. Fog out of the slough and horses
asleep in the barn. In the field, sparrow hawks
Glittered through the morning clouds.

No dreamers knew the rain. Wind ruffled quills
in the mongrel's nose. He sighed cautiously,
kicked further beneath the weathered shed and slept.

Timid chickens watched chickens in the puddles.
Watching the chickens, yellow eyes harsh
below the wind-drifting clouds, sparrow hawks.

Horses stamped in the barn. The mongrel whimpered
in his dream, wind ruffled his mongrel tail,
the lazy cattails and the rain.

The Cellist to His Dog

Warren Wigutow

My dark tones let them ring in the halls of Cynopolis
Set is there to tap time and you my friend bay
bay so that we are heard
the maestro even across time will hear such an ensemble
Salvatore Lanzetti in Sardibia   Canvasso   Ferrari
O blessed Handel your obbligato   there am I in a row
one voice   deeper than the rest   richer and richer
in the audience   dogs   not such as yourself
Feuermann   but well-bred ticket holders   coughing
and snoring   applauding between movements
alone here   BWV 1007 begins it   Prelude
in the street a girl screams but then laughs I can feel
the vibration   Allemande   in the tail-pin   your
tail thumps against my extended knee   Courante
my heart breaks again   again   Sara   Sara
Sarabande   the evening bus arrives and as the doors
close   so too close   Menuett   lighter still
my eyes   Gigue   useless in their sockets   my eyes
Feuermann   lead me to the corner   where in a haze
of cigar smoke   we will listen   you and I
to the far away sound of heaven   a car radio   is it
Elgar?   for you a bark in the distance   for me
always Bach   Six Suites   where I touch   an
angel informs my hands   my old hands   trace your
profile   Feuermann   in relief   upon a stone
temple wall   hems-a em t'esert   I sit in the pupil
of the
eye

THE PARDON

RICHARD WILBUR

My dog lay dead five days without a grave
In the thick of summer, hid in a clump of pine
And a jungle of grass and honeysuckle-vine.
I who had loved him while he kept alive

Went only close enough to where he was
To sniff the heavy honeysuckle-smell
Twined with another odor heavier still
And hear the flies' intolerable buzz.

Well, I was ten and very much afraid.
In my kind world the dead were out of range
And I could not forgive the sad or strange
In beast or man. My father took the spade

And buried him. Last night I saw the grass
Slowly divide (it was the same scene
But now it glowed a fierce and mortal green)
And saw the dog emerging. I confess

I felt afraid again, but still he came
In the carnal sun, clothed in a hymn of flies,
And death was breeding in his lively eyes.
I started in to cry and call his name,

Asking forgiveness of his tongueless head.
. . . I dreamt the past was never past redeeming:
But whether this was false or honest dreaming
I beg death's pardon now. And mourn the dead.

THE DOG

C. K. WILLIAMS

Except for the dog, that she wouldn't have him put away, wouldn't let
  him die, I'd have liked her.
She was handsome, busty, chunky, early middle-aged, very black, with
  a stiff, exotic dignity
that flurried up in me a mix of warmth and sexual apprehension neither
  of which, to tell the truth,
I tried very hard to nail down: she was that much older and in those
  days there was still the race thing.
This was just at the time of civil rights: the neighborhood I was living
  in was mixed.
In the narrow streets, the tiny three-floored houses they called father-
  son-holy-ghosts
which had been servants' quarters first, workers' tenements, then slums,
  still were, but enclaves of us,
beatniks and young artists, squatted there and commerce between
  everyone was fairly easy.
Her dog, a grinning mongrel, rib and knob, gristle and grizzle, wasn't
  terribly offensive.
The trouble was that he was ill, or the trouble more exactly was that I
  had to know about it.
She used to walk him on a lot I overlooked, he must have had a tumor
  or a blockage of some sort
because every time he moved his bowels, he shrieked, a chilling, almost
  human scream of anguish.
It nearly always caught me unawares, but even when I'd see them first,
  it wasn't better.
The limp leash coiled in her hand, the woman would be profiled to the
  dog, staring into the distance,
apparently oblivious, those breasts of hers like stone, while he, not a
  step away, laboring,
trying to eject the feeble, mucus-coated, blood-flecked chains that finally
  spurted from him,

would set himself on tip-toe and hump into a question mark, one
    quivering back leg grotesquely lifted.
Every other moment he'd turn his head, as though he wanted her, to
    no avail, to look at him,
then his eyes would dim and he'd drive his wounded anus in the dirt,
    keening uncontrollably,
lurching forward in a hideous, electric dance as though someone were
    at him with a club.
When at last he'd finish, she'd wipe him with a tissue like a child; he'd
    lick her hand.
It was horrifying; I was always going to call the police; once I actually
    went out to chastise her—
didn't she know how selfish she was, how the animal was suffering?—
    She scared me off, though.
She was older than I'd thought, for one thing, her flesh was loosening,
    pouches of fat beneath the eyes,
and poorer, too, shabby, tarnished: I imagined smelling something
    faintly acrid as I passed.
Had I every really mooned for such a creature? I slunk around the
    block, chagrined, abashed.
I don't recall them too long after that. Maybe the dog died, maybe I
    was just less sensitive.
Maybe one year when the cold came and I closed my windows, I forgot
    them . . . then I moved.
Everything was complicated now, so many tensions, so much
    bothersome self-consciousness.
Anyway, those back streets, especially in bad weather when the ginkgos
    lost their leaves, were bleak.
It's restored there now, ivy, pointed brick, garden walls with broken
    bottles mortared on them,
but you'd get sick and tired then: the rubbish in the gutter, the general
    sense of dereliction.
Also, I'd found a girl to be in love with: all we wanted was to live
    together, so we did.

To a Dog Injured in the Street

William Carlos Williams

It is myself,
    not the poor beast lying there
             yelping with pain
that brings me to myself with a start—
    as at the explosion
             of a bomb, a bomb that has laid
all the world to waste.
    I can do nothing
             but sing about it
and so I am assuaged
    from my pain.

A drowsy numbness drowns my sense
    as if of hemlock
             I had drunk. I think
of the poetry
    of René Char
             and all he must have seen
and suffered
    that has brought him
             to speak only of
sedgy rivers,
    of daffodils and tulips
             whose roots they water,
even to the free-flowing river
    that laves the rootlets
             of those sweet-scented flowers
that people the
    milky
             way

I remember Norma
                our English setter of my childhood
                            her silky ears
and expressive eyes.
        She had a litter
                        of pups one night
in our pantry and I kicked
        one of them
                        thinking, in my alarm,
that they
        were biting her breasts
                        to destroy her.

I remember also
        a dead rabbit
                        lying harmlessly
on the outspread palm
        of a hunter's hand.
                        As I stood by
watching
        he took a hunting knife
                        and with a laugh
thrust it
        up into the animal's private parts.
                        I almost fainted.

Why should I think of that now?
        The cries of a dying dog
                        are to be blotted out
as best I can.
        René Char
                        you are a poet who believes
in the power of beauty
        to right all wrongs.
                        I believe it also.
With invention and courage
        we shall surpass

> the pitiful dumb beasts,
> let all men believe it,
> as you have taught me also
> to believe it.

THE DOG POISONER

KEITH WILSON

To this day, no one knows who he was or she was.
All we kids knew was that it came in the night,
little balls of hamburger (Then you could buy it,
three pounds for a quarter. My mother made me tell
the butcher it was for my dog, but we ate it.)
came over the fence, lay there and real soon
a dog lay there, writhing in pain. Ground glass

was all it ever used and we hated it, would I'm sure
have killed it if we could ever have caught it.
Forgive me for saying "it," but who could think
of such a creature as an animal or even a human?
My mother said once what it really wanted was to kill
a human, a boy or a girl, but hadn't enough courage.

We boys finally banded together and patrolled the huge
vacant lots that separated our homes but all we ever
got was tired and our parents made us stop, even though
the killings went on.
                    One day they just quit. It happened
that the day before an old man who lived down towards
the Valley got sick and died, vomiting blood.
The doc said he didn't know what killed him
but we did. He got his hamburger mixed up and
God forgive me, we were so glad we got out
and danced in a circle, shouting as if it were
raining or some other miracle had happened.

DOG

CHARLES WRIGHT

The fantailed dog of the end, the lights out,
Lopes in his sleep,
The moon's moan in the glassy fields.
Everything comes to him, stone
Pad prints extending like stars, tongue black
As a flag, saliva and thread, the needle's tooth,
Everything comes to him.

If I were wind, which I am, if I
Were smoke, which I am, if I
Were the colorless leaves, the invisible grief,
Which I am, which I am,
He'd whistle me down, and down, but not yet.

DOG IN A CORNFIELD

JAMES WRIGHT

Fallow between the horny trees
  The empty field
Lay underneath the motions of the cloud.
My master called for bobwhites on his knees,
  And suddenly the wind revealed
The body pitching forward in the mud.

My master leaped alive at first,
  And cried, and ran
Faster than air could echo feet and hands.
The lazy maples wailed beyond the crust
  Of earth and artificial man.
Here lay one death the autumn understands.

How could I know he ran to lie,
  And joke with me,
Beside the toppled scarecrow there, as though
His body, like the straw, lay beaten dry?
  Growling, I circled near a tree,
Indifferent to a solitary crow.

Down on the stubble field the pair
  Lay side by side,
Scarecrow and master. I could barely tell
Body from body, and the color of hair
  Blended, to let my master hide.
His laughter thickened like a droning bell.

I called him out of earth, to come
  And walk with me,
To leave that furrow where the man's shape broke,
To let the earth collapse, and come on home.

The limber scarecrow knew the way
To meet the wind, that monumental joke;

But once the real man tumbled down,
    Funny or not,
The broomstick and the straw might leap and cry.
Scared of the chance to wrestle wood and stone,
    I howled into the air, forgot
How scarecrows stumble in a field to die.

Snarling, I leaped the rusty fence,
    I ran across
The shock of leaves, blundering as I tore
Into the scarecrow in the man's defense.
    My master rolled away on grass
And saw me scatter legs and arms in air.

And saw me summon all my force
    To shake apart
The brittle shoes, the tough blades of the brains
Back to the ground; the brutal formlessness,
    The twisted knot of its arid heart
Back to the sweet roots of autumn rain.

Where do the sticks and stones get off,
    Mocking the shape
Of eyes younger than summer, of thoughtful hands?
The real man falls to nothing fast enough.
    I barked into the air, to keep
The man quick to a joy he understands.

THE OLD DOG IN THE RUINS OF THE GRAVES AT ARLES

JAMES WRIGHT

I have heard tell somewhere,
Or read, I forget which,
That animals tumble along in a forever,
A little dream, a quick longing
For every fine haunch that passes,
As the young bitches glitter in their own light.

I find their freedom from lonely wisdom
Hard to believe.
No matter the brief skull fails to contain,
The old bones know something.

Almost indistinguishable from the dust,
They seek shadow, they limp among the tombs.
One stray mutt, long since out of patience,
Rises up, as the sunlight happens to strike,
And snaps at his right foreleg.

When the hurrying shadow returns
He lies down in peace again,
Between the still perfectly formed sarcophagi
That have been empty of Romans or anybody
Longer than anybody remembers.
Graves last longer than men. Nobody can tell me
The old dogs don't know.

THE DOGS OF ZIMMER

PAUL ZIMMER

The tether of the aeons holds them.
There is order and habit in their love.
But sometimes they turn on each other
In frustration, snarling and flashing teeth.
On moonlit nights they grow restless,
Hearing things they cannot see.
They chew on pillows, wet the rugs.

A busy man should have perfect dogs,
But Zimmer's dogs go flick, flick, flick,
Moaning and thumping the floorboards.
They tongue his hand in the night
And make him get up to pee.

Sometimes when he unchains them,
They whisk away before he can call
Them back. He does not know
Where they go or what they do.
He spends hours wistfully calling them,
Imagines how they snuffle post holes,
Raise their dingy hinders to great stones
Or tunnel into ancient graves.

But always when it seems worst,
That they have gone wild into the woods,
Joining packs to overrun the suburbs,
It's flick, flick, flick outside his windows,
And Zimmer opens to see them smiling.
The wild lights in their eyes grown dim,
They bang the doorway with their tails.

SONG OF THE BLACK DOG

PAUL ZIMMER

When my black dog sings,
Her eyes distant and longing,
She reaches high into her art,
Becoming light and air,
Throat held straight open and true
To the depth of her feeling.

Her sweet pitch, rising
To the far corners of the house
And out the window screens,
Move the squirrels to thump
And scramble on the roof,
Scrolling themselves as they flit
Away through gossamer and twigs.

Her fine songs make big birds
Fan out of the meadow,
Whomping into air,
And little creatures scurry
To their brush piles.
Even the bones of a dead deer
In the south woods almost rise
In alarm to clatter away.

PERMISSIONS AND COPYRIGHTS

The editors have made every effort to locate the owners of copyrighted material and to secure permission to reprint. Permission to reprint poems is gratefully acknowledged to the following:

Pamela Alexander. "The Dog at the Center of the Universe" from *Navigable Waterways* (1985), Yale University Press. Used by permission. "Consolation" from *Commonwealth of Wings*. Copyright © 1991 by Pamela Alexander, permission by the University Press of New England.

John Allman. "The Dog" and "Running" from *Scenarios for a Mixed Landscape*. Copyright © 1986 by John Allman. Reprinted by permission of New Directions Publishing Corp.

Yehuda Amichai. "A Dog after Love" from *Amen*, Harper & Row Publishing Co., copyright © 1977 by Yehuda Amichai. Used by permission of the author.

Jon Anderson. "Ye Bruthers Dogg" from *In Sepia*, copyright © 1974 by Jon Anderson.

Anonymous. "Old Blue," traditional. In the public domain. Collected during the first half of the century and generally thought to have originated in Mississippi. The lyrics quoted here are taken from Joan Baez's recording of the song on her album "Joan Baez, Vol. 2," Vanguard VSD-2097. For lyrical variations and further background, see *The 111 Best American Ballads: Folk Song USA*, Alan Lomax, ed., New York, Duell, Sloan & Pearce, Inc., 1947; *Folksongs of Mississippi and Their Background*, Arthur Palmer Hudson, ed., New York and Philidelphia, FOLKLORICA, 1981; *Ozark Folksons, Vol II: Songs of the South and West*, Vance Randolph, ed., Columbia, University of Missouri Press, 1980.

Anonymous (Pima Indian). "Dog Son," version by Joseph Duemer, copyright © 1996 by Joseph Duemer. Used by permission of the author. (Original translation by Frank Russell.)

Sondra Audin Armer. "The Dogs," copyright © 1990 Sondra Audin Armer, used by permission of the author.

Renee Ashley. "The Last Night You Are Gone" from *Salt*, winner of the Brittingham Prize in Poetry. Copyright © 1991 (Madison: The University of Wisconsin Press). "Lost Dogs" from *Southern Poetry Review*, copyright © 1993.

Jeff Avants. "Dog's Tale" from *Testament*, copyright © 1991 by Jeff Avants. Used by permission of the author.

David Baker. "Sunbathing" from *Sweet Home, Saturday Night* (University of Arkansas Press, 1991), copyright © 1991 by David Baker. Used by permission of the author.

Angela Ball. "Phantom Dog." Copyright © 1996 by Angela Ball. Used by permission of the author.

Robin Becker. "Giacometti's Dog" from *Giacometti's Dog*, copyright © 1990 by Robin Becker. Used by permission of the author.

Marck L. Beggs. "Kilty Sue" from *Manhattan Poetry Review*, copyright © 1989 by Marck L. Beggs. Use by permission of the author.

Marvin Bell. "The Book of the Dead Man (#68)," copyright © 1996 by Marvin Bell. Used by permission of the author. "Wherever You Are" from *Segues: A Correspondence in Poetry* by Marvin Bell and William Stafford, Godine 1983. Used by permission of Marvin Bell.

David Biespiel. "Walking with Virgil" copyright © 1994 by David Biespiel. Used by permission of the author.

Elizabeth Bishop. "Pink Dog" from *The Complete Poems 1927–1979* by Elizabeth Bishop. Copyright © 1979, 1983 by Alice Helen Methfessel. Reprinted by permission of Farrar, Straus & Giroux, Inc.

Cathy Smith Bowers. "Losses" from *The Love that Ended Yesterday in Texas* (Texas Tech. University Press), copyright © 1992 by Texas Tech. University Press. Used by permission of the author.

Kay Boyle. "The Lost Dogs of Phnom Penh," copyright © 1991. Reprinted by permission of the author and the Watkins/Loomis Agency.

William Bronk. "The Subsidy" from *Life Supports*, copyright © 1981 by William Bronk. Used by permission of the author.

Charles Bukowski. "dogfight" copyright © 1974 by Charles Bukowski. Reprinted from *Burning in Water, Drowning in Flame: Selected Poems 1955–1973* with the permission of Black Sparrow Press.

Michael Burkard. "The Dogs on the Cliffs" from *The Fires They Kept*, copyright © 1986 by Michael Burkhard. Used by permission of the author.

Thomas Carper. "A Guardian Tanya" and "Jogging with Tanya" from *Fiddle Lane*, the Johns Hopkins University Press (Baltimore & London), copyright © 1991. "A Guardian Tanya" first appeared in *Poetry*, July 1990.

Hayden Carruth. "Haiku" copyright © 1965 by Hayden Carruth. "Underground the Darkness is the Light" from *Tell Me Again How the White Heron Rises and Flies Across the Nacreous River at Twilight Toward the Distant Islands*. Copyright © 1986 by Hayden Carruth. Reprinted by permission of New Directions Publishing Corp.

Raymond Carver. "Your Dog Dies," copyright © 1976 by Tess Gallagher. Reprinted by permission of International Creative Management, Inc.

Siv Cedering. "Because the Dog Demands" copyright © 1996 by Siv Cedering. "Dog Days" is reprinted from *Letters from the Floating World*, by permission of the University of Pittsburgh Press. Copyright © by Siv Cedering.

Marilyn Chin. "After My Last Paycheck . . ." from *Dwarf Bamboo* (Greenfield Review Press), copyright © 1987 by Marilyn Chin. Used by permission of the author.

David Citino. "Homage to Our Lady of the Strays," first published in *The Laurel Review.* Copyright © 1991 by David Citino, used by permission of the author.

Robin Clark. "If Joan of Arc Had a Dog," copyright © 1994 by Robin Clark. Used by permission of the author.

William Clipman. "Dog Light" from *Dog Light* (Wesleyan University Press), copyright © 1981 by William Clipman. Used by permission of the author.

Billy Collins. "Dog" from *Questions about Angels* (William Morrow & Co.), copyright © 1991 by Billy Collins. Used by permission of the author. "RCA Victor" from *The Apple that Astonished Paris* (Applezaba Press), copyright © 1980 by Billy Collins. Used by permission of the author.

Henri Coulette. "In the 9th Year of the Literary War" and "Night Thoughts" from *The Collected Poems of Henri Coulette* (Donald Justice and Robert Meazy, editors), The University of Arkansas Press, copyright © 1990.

Mark Cox. "The Word" from *Smoulder*, reprinted by permission of David R. Godine, Publisher, Inc., copyright © 1989 by Mark Cox. "History" copyright © 1992 by Mark Cox. Used by permission of the author.

Mary Crow. "Crying Wolf" originally published in *Nimrod*, 1995. Copyright © 1995 by Mary Crow. Used by permission of the author.

Robert Dana. "Dog Music," copyright © 1994 by Robert Dana. Used by permission of the author.

James Dickey. "A Dog Sleeping on My Feet" from *Poetry* (January 1962); from *Drowning with Others* (1962); reprinted in *Poems 1957–1967* (1967), *The Early Motion* (1981), Wesleyan University Press and *The Whole Motion*, Wesleyan University Press of New England (1992). Used by permission of James Dickey.

William Dickey. Leonard Sanzaro, Executor for the estate of William Dickey for "Dog Under False Pretenses" *In Dreaming: Selected Poems* by William Dickey, copyright © 1994, University of Arkansas Press. "Hope" from *More Under Saturn*, Wesleyan University Press. Used by permission of Leonard Sanzaro, Executor of the estate of William Dickey.

Stephen Dobyns. "How to Like It" from *Cemetary Nights*. Copyright © 1987 by Stephen Dobyns. Used by permission of Viking Penguin, a division of Penguin Books USA, Inc.

Stephen Dowdall. "Two Dogs," copyright © 1996 by Stephen Dowdall, used by permission of the author.

Joseph Duemer, "Dogs at Dog Beach" from *Customs*, copyright © 1987 by Joseph Duemer. Used by permission of the University of Georgia Press and Joseph Duemer.

Stephen Dunn. "Something like Happiness." Reprinted by permission of Stephen Dunn and W. W. Norton & Co., Inc., from *New and Selected Poems: 1974–1994* by Stephen Dunn. Copyright © 1994 by Stephen Dunn.

Russell Edson. "The Dog's Music" from *Clam Theater* (Wesleyan University Press), copyright © 1973 by Russell Edson. Used by permission of the author. "The Dog" from *The Intuitive Journey and Other Works* (Harper & Row), copyright © 1976 by Russell Edson. Used by permission of the author.

Ron Ezzie. "Afternoon Walk," copyright © 1996 by Ron Ezzie, used by permission of the author.

Lawrence Ferlinghetti. "Dog" from *A Coney Island of the Mind*. Copyright © 1958 by Lawrence Ferlinghetti. Reprinted by permission of New Directions Publishing Corp.

Donald Finkel. "Hound Song" from *What Manner of Beast*, copyright © 1981 by Donald Finkel. Used by permission of the author.

Carol Frost. "The New Dog" from *Day of the Body*, copyright © 1986 by Carol Frost. Use by permission of the author.

Richard Frost. "Kisses," first published in *Raccoon* No. 17, copyright © 1985 by Richard Frost. Used by permission of the author.

Reyes Garcia. "Black Dog, River, Moon" first appeared in *The Denver Quarterly*, copyright © 1994 by Reyes Garcia.

Michael Gessner. "Lines on a Dog's Face" first published in *Oxford Magazine*, copyright © 1993 by Michael Gessner. Used by permission of the author.

Louise Glück. "The Gift" and "Rosy" from *Descending Figure*, Ecco Press, copyright © 1980 by Lousie Glück. Used by permission of the author.

Albert Goldbarth. "Married in the Presence of the Lord" and "Water Pie: Tonight, 12/11/72" from *Jan 31*, Doubleday and Co., copyright © 1974 by Albert Goldbarth. Used by permission of the author.

David Graham. "Bad Dogs" from *Doggedness*, Devil's Millhopper Press, copyright © 1989 by Devil's Millhopper Press. Used by permission of the author.

Thom Gunn. "Her Pet" from *The Man with Night Sweats*. Copyright © 1994 by Thom Gunn. Reprinted by permission of Faber and Faber Ltd. Reprinted in the United States by permission of Farrar, Straus & Giroux, Inc.

Rachel Hadas. "Getting Rid of the Dog by Taking It around the Mountain" from *Slow Transparency*, copyright © 1983 by Rachel Hadas, Wesleyan University Press. Used by permission of University Press of New England.

Sidney Hall Jr. "Lazy Sleeping Dogs" from *What We Will Give Each Other*, copyright © 1993 by Sidney Hall Jr. Used by permission of the author.

254

Michael S. Harper. "Sandra: At the Beaver Trap," copyright © 1972 by Michael S. Harper. Used by permission of the author.

William Hathaway. "This Tree," from *Looking into the Heart of Light*, copyright © 1988 by William Hathaway, University of Central Florida Press. Used by permission of the author.

H. L. Hix. "Lament for the Feet" from *New Mexico Humanities Review*, copyright © 1991 by H. L. Hix. Used by permission of the author.

Linda Hogan. "Bear Fat" from *Book of Medicines*, Coffee House Press, copyright © 1993. Used by permission of the author.

Anselm Hollo. "Pygmy Hut" from *Outlying Districts*, Coffee House Press, copyright © 1990 by Anselm Hollo. Used by permission of the author. "*from* Some Worlds" from *Sojourner Microcosms*, Blue Wind Press, copyright © 1977 by Anselm Hollo. Used by permission of the author.

Miroslav Holub. "On the Dog Angel" from *Sagital Section*, Field Translation Series, copyright © 1980 by Oberlin College. Translated by Stuart Friebert and Dana Hábová. Used by permission of the editors of *Field* and Oberlin College.

Christopher Howell. "Like Feelings" and "This Afterward" from *Deep Down Things: Poems of the Inland Pacific Northwest*, copyright © 1990 by Christopher Howell. Used by permission of the author.

Richard Jackson. "About the Dogs of Dachau" from *Alive All Day*, Cleveland State University Press, copyright © 1992 by Richard Jackson. Used by permission of the author.

Stan James. "Dogs at a Concert" copyright © 1984 by Stan James. Used by permission of the author.

Donald Justice. "The Stray Dog by the Summerhouse" from *The Summer Anniversaries* by Donald Justice, copyright © 1981 by Donald Justice. Used by permission of the author.

Richard Katrovas. "A Dog and a Boy" from *Snug Harbor*, Wesleyan University Press, copyright © 1986 by Richard Katrovas. Used by permission of the author.

Weldon Kees. "Dog" reprinted from *The Collected Poems of Weldon Kees*, edited by Donald Justice, by permission of the University of Nebraska Press. Copyright © 1975 by the University of Nebraska Press.

Brigit Pegeen Kelly. "Harmony Stoneworks, Late Winter" and "Dog" from *To the Place of Trumpets* by Brigit Pegeen Kelly, Yale University Press, copyright © 1988 by Yale University Press. Used by permission of the author and Yale University Press.

Mary Kinzie. "Taffy" first published in *Salmagundi* (1990), copyright © 1990 by Mary Kinzie. Used by permission of the author.

Maxine Kumin. "Custodian" copyright © 1988 by Maxine Kumin, from *Nurture* by Maxine Kumin. Used by permission of Viking Penguin, a division of Penguin Books USA Inc.

Greg Kuzma. "Where the Dogs Lie Down with the Cats" first published in *Kansas Quarterly* (1989), copyright © 1989 by Greg Kuzma. "The Return" copyright © 1995 by Greg Kuzma. Used by permission of the author.

Sydney Lea. "The Wrong Way Will Haunt You (Shooting a Hound)," and "Instructions: The Dog (Ray Speaks)" from *The Floating Candles*, University of Illinois, Urbana, copyright © 1982 by the University of Illinois, Urbana. Used by permission of the author.

Denise Levertov. "The Dog of Art" from *Collected Earlier Poems 1940–1960.* Copyright © 1959 by Denise Levertov. Reprinted by permission of New Directions Publishing Corp. Reprinted in Britain by permission of Laurence Pollinger Ltd.

Philip Levine. "Dog Poem" from *A Walk with Tom Jefferson*, Alfred A. Knopf, Inc., copyright © 1988 by Philip Levine. Used by permission of the author.

Thomas Lux. "So You Put the Dog to Sleep" from *The Drowned River*, Houghton Mifflin Co., copyright © 1990 by Thomas Lux. Used by permission of the author.

Thomas McAfee. "The Mongrel Dog and I" first appeared in *I'll Be Home Late Tonight*, University of Missouri Press, copyright 1967 by Thomas McAfee. Reprinted by permission of McAfee Literary Estate c/o *The Missouri Review.*

Martha McFerren. "A Metaphor Crosses the Road" from *Women in Cars* by Martha McFerren. Copyright © 1992 by Martha McFerren. Reprinted with permission from Helicon Nine Editions.

Thomas McGrath. "In August" from *The Movie at the End of the World: Collected Poems*, by Thomas McGrath, Ohio University Press/ Swallow Press, copyright © 1972.

Freya Manfred. "The Dog in the Bar-Room Mirror" from *American Roads* by Freya Manfred, copyright © 1979 by Overlook Press, Inc. Used by permission of the author.

Paul Mariani. "Lines I Told Myself I Wouldn't Write" from *Prime Mover* by Paul Mariani, copyright © 1985 by Paul Mariani. "Landscape with Dog" from *Shadow Portraits* by Paul Mariani, copyright © 1995 by Paul Mariani. Used by permission of the author.

William Matthews. "Homer's Seeing-Eye Dog" from *Blues if You Want*, copyright © 1989 by William Matthews. Reprinted by permission of Houghton Mifflin Co. All rights reserved. "Loyal" from *A Happy Childhood*, copyright © 1985 by William Matthews. Used by permission of the author.

James Merrill. "The Victor Dog" from *Braving the Elements*, copyright © 1972 by James Merrill. Reprinted by permission of Alfred A. Knopf, Inc.

W. S. Merwin. "Ali" reprinted from *Opening the Hand*, Athaneum, copyright © 1983 W. S. Merwin. Used by permission of the author.

Giles Mitchell. "Elephant, Dog, River" copyright © 1996 Giles Mitchell. Used by permission of the author.

Michael Moos. "Falling Dog" first appeared in *North Dakota Quarterly* (1991), copyright © 1991 by the University of North Dakota. Used by permission of the author.

Donald Morrill. "The Throes" copyright © 1996 by Donald Morrill. Used by permission of the author.

Lisel Mueller. "What the Dog Perhaps Hears" from *The Private Life*, by Lisel Mueller. Copyright © 1976 by the author, published by Louisiana State University Press. Used with permission.

Joan Murray. "The Black Dog: On Being a Poet" copyright © 1996 by Joan Murray. Used by permission of the author.

Jack Myers. "Arf" from *As Long As You're Happy*, by Jack Myers, copyright © 1986, Graywolf Press. Used by permission of the author.

Howard Nemerov. "Walking the Dog" from *Sentences* (1980); reprinted in *Trying Conclusions: Poems 1961–1991*, University of Chicago Press, copyright © 1991 by the estate of Howard Nemerov. Reprinted by permission of Mrs. Howard Nemerov.

Greg Pape. "The Dogs of Chinle" from *Storm Pattern*, University of Pittsburgh Press, copyright © 1992 by Greg Pape. Used by permission of the author.

Robert Parham. "Why Pets Run The World" copyright © 1994 by Robert Parham. Used by permission of the author.

Michael Pettit. "Pavlov's Dog" reprinted from *Cardinal Points* by Michael Pettit, copyright © 1987 by Michael Pettit. Used by permission of the University of Iowa Press.

Michael Pfeifer. " 'Coon Dogs" copyright © 1980 by Michael Pfeifer. Used by permission of the author.

Stanley Plumly. "Panegyric for Gee" first appeared in *Antaeus: The Final Issue* (1994), copyright © 1994 by Stanley Plumly. Used by permission of the author.

Lawrence Raab. "Bad Dog" from *What We Don't Know About Each Other* by Lawrence Raab. Copyright © 1993 by Lawrence Raab. Used by permission of Viking Penguin, a division of Penguin Books USA Inc.

Carl Rakosi. "To a Collie Pup" from *Collected Poems* by Carl Rakoski, copyright © 1986 by Callman Rawley. Used by permission of the author.

Bin Ramke. "Death of a Dog" from "Secrets of the Saints" from *The Difference Between Night and Day* by Bin Ramke (Yale University Press), copyright © 1978 by Bin Ramke. Used by permission of the author.

David Ray. "Dog" and "The Old Dog" copyright © 1996 by David Ray. Used by permission of the author.

Adrienne Rich. "This" from *Time's Power: Poems 1985–1988* by Adrienne Rich. Copyright © 1989 by Adrienne Rich. Reprinted by permission of the author and W. W. Norton & Company, Inc.

Boyer Rickel. "Poem to Begin the Second Decade of AIDS" from *Arreboles*, copyright © 1991 by Boyer Rickel, Wesleyan University Press. Used by permission of the University Press of New England.

Michael J. Rosen. "Trying to Write You a Poem . . ." first appeared in *NER/BLQ*, copyright © 1992 by Michael J. Rosen. Used by permission of the author.

Liz Rosenberg. "Elegy for a Beagle Mutt" from *The Fire Music* (University of Pittsburgh Press), copyright © 1986 by the University of Pittsburgh Press. Used by permission of the author. "Susquehanna" from *Children of Paradise*, by Liz Rosenberg, copyright © 1994 by Liz Rosenberg. Reprinted by permission of the University of Pittsburgh Press.

Dennis Schmitz. "The Three-Legged Dog" first appeared in *Hayden's Ferry Review* (1988), copyright © 1988 by Dennis Schmitz. Used by permission of the author.

James Seay. "My Dog and I Grow Fat" from *Let Not Your Hart*, copyright © 1970 by James Seay, Wesleyan University Press. Used by permission of the author.

Brenda Shaw. "Living Snow," from *Gallimaufry* (Scotland, UK). Copyright © 1986 by Brenda Shaw. Used by permission of the author.

Charles Simic. "Country Fair" from *Hotel Insomnia*. Copyright © 1994 by Charles Simic. Used by permission of Harcourt Brace & Co.

Jim Simmerman. "Maddy's Woods" from *Moon Go Away, I Don't Love You No More* (Miami University Press) by Jim Simmerman, copyright © 1994 by Jim Simmerman. "Fetch" first appeared in *Poetry*, 1985 from *Once Out of Nature* (Galileo Press) by Jim Simmerman, copyright © 1989 by Jim Simmerman. Used by permission of the author.

Maurya Simon. "Bark with Authority" first published in *The Spoon River Poetry Review* (1994), copyright © 1994 by Maurya Simon. Used by permission of the author.

William Stafford. "How It Began" from *A Glass Face in the Rain*, copyright © 1983 the Estate of William Stafford. Used by permission of Kim Stafford, Executor of the Estate of William Stafford. "Dear Marvin," from *Segues*, copyright © 1983 the Estate of William Stafford. Used by permission of Kim Stafford, Executor of the Estate of William Stafford, and Marvin Bell.

Frank Stanford. "The Wolves" from *You*, copyright © 1979 the Estate of Frank Stanford.

Gerald Stern. "Love for the Dog" from *Lucky Life*, copyright © 1977 by Gerald Stern. Used by permission of the author. "The Dog" from *Love Sick*, copyright © 1988 by Gerald Stern. Used by permission of the author.

258

Frank Stewart. "The Black Moth" first appeared in *Floating Island* (1989), copyright ©
1989 by Frank Stewart. Reprinted by permission of the author.

Pamela Stewart. "Dogs, Her Dreaming" from *Prairie Schooner* copyright © 1995 by the
University of Nebraska Press. Used by permission of the University of Nebraska Press.
"Newfoundland-Praise" copyright © 1996 by Pamela Stewart. Used by permission of the
author.

Robert Sward. "Uncle Dog: The Poet at 9" first published in *The Chicago Review*. Reprinted
here from *Four Incarnations, New and Selected Poems*, Coffee House Press. Copyright ©
1957–1994 by Robert Sward. Reprinted with permission of the author. "Clancy the Dog"
reprinted from *Four Incarnations, New and Selected Poems*, Coffee House Press. Copyright
© 1957–1994 by Robert Sward. Reprinted by permission of the author.

Suntaro Tanikawa. "Dog" and "August and February" copyright © 1983 Harold Wright.
Reprinted by permission of Bonnie R. Crown.

Elizabeth Marshall Thomas. "Pearl and I Are Far Too Fat" copyright © 1996 by Elizabeth
Marshall Thomas. Used by permission of the author.

John Updike. "Dog's Death" from the *Collected Poems of John Updike*, copyright © 1994
by John Updike. Reprinted by permission of Alfred A. Knopf, Inc. Reprinted in Britain
by permission of Penguin Books, Ltd.

Gloria Vando. "Divine Right" copyright © 1996 by Gloria Vando. Used by permission
of the author.

Ellen Bryant Voigt. "Nightshade" and "The Trust" from *The Lotus Flowers: Poems by
Ellen Bryant Voigt*, copyright © 1987 by Ellen Bryant Voigt. Reprinted by permission of
Ellen Bryant Voigt and W. W. Norton & Company, Inc.

Nancy B. Wall. "Old Dog" copyright © 1994 by Nancy B. Wall. Used by permission of
the author.

Michael Waters. "Dogs in the Storm" first appeared in the *Antioch Review*. Reprinted
from *Anniversary of the Air*, by Michael Waters, copyright © 1985 by Michael Waters,
published by Carnegie Mellon University Press. Used by permission of the author. "Village
Dogs" first appeared in *The Ohio Review*. Reprinted from *Bountiful*, by Michael Waters,
copyright © 1992 by Michael Waters, published by Carnegie Mellon University Press.
Used by permission of the author.

Bruce Weigl. "May" copyright © 1992 Bruce Weigl. Used by permission of the author.
"Dogs" first appeared in *The Monkey Wars* (University of Georgia Press), copyright ©
1984 by Bruce Weigl. Used by permission of the author.

James Welch. "Day after Chasing Porcupines" is reprinted from *Riding the Earthboy 40*
by James Welch. Copyright © 1971, 1976, 1990 by James Welch. Reprinted by permission
of Confluence Press at Lewis-Clark State College, Lewiston, Idaho.

Warren Wigutow. "The Cellist to His Dog" first appeared in *Notus*. Reprinted from *Men & Women: Ten Phantasies for Robert Browning*, copyright © 1996 Warren Wigutow. Used by permission of the author.

Richard Wilbur. "The Pardon" from *Ceremony and Other Poems*, copyright © 1950 and renewed 1978 by Richard Wilbur, reprinted by permission of Harcourt Brace & Company.

C. K. Williams. "The Dog" from *Poems 1963–1983* by C. K. Williams, Farrar, Straus & Giroux, copyright © 1983, 1988 by C. K. Williams. Reprinted by permission of Farrar, Straus & Giroux.

William Carlos Williams. "To a Dog Injured in the Street" from *Collected Poems 1939–1962*, volume II. Copyright © 1953 by William Carlos Williams. Reprinted by permission of New Directions Publishing Corp. Reprinted in Britain by permission of Carcanet Press, Ltd.

Keith Wilson. "The Dog Poisoner" copyright © 1989 by Keith Wilson. All rights reserved. Used by permission of the author.

Charles Wright. "Dog" from *Country Music*, copyright © 1991 by Charles Wright, Wesleyan University Press, by permission of the University Press of New England. Used by permission of the author.

James Wright. "Dog in a Cornfield" from *Saint Judas*, copyright © 1959 by James Wright, Wesleyan University Press by permission of the University Press of New England. "The Old Dog in the Ruins of the Graves at Arles" from *Above the River*, by James Wright. Copyright © 1990 by Anne Wright. Reprinted by permission of Farrar, Straus & Girous, Inc.

Paul Zimmer. "The Dogs of Zimmer" is reprinted from *Family Reunion*, by Paul Zimmer, by permission of the University of Pittsburgh Press. Copyright © 1983 by Paul Zimmer. "Song of the Black Dog" reprinted by permission of the University of Arkansas from *Big Blue Train*, by Paul Zimmer, copyright © 1993.

About the Contributors

PAMELA ALEXANDER's two poetry collections are *Navigable Waterways* (Yale) and *A Commonwealth of Wings* (Univ. Press of New England, 1991). She teaches creative writing at MIT.

JOHN ALLMAN's collections of poetry include *Scenarios for a Mixed Landscape* and *Curve Away from Stillness* (New Directions). His first collection of stories, *Descending Fire and Other Stories*, was published in 1994 by New Directions.

YEHUDA AMICHAI was born in Germany in 1924. In 1936, he emigrated with his family to Israel. He saw active service on the Negev front in the Israeli War of Independence and later in the Sinai Campaign. His numerous collections of poetry and short fiction have been published in both Israel and the United States.

JON ANDERSON writes, "Finding themselves imprisoned in a rather small yard in Portland, Oregon, in 1970, Hodain (German shepherd) & Toolie (Newfoundland Labrador) endeavored to escape by digging a hole beneath the fence. They disguised their efforts thusly: whenever a human stepped out of the house, one of them would lie in the hole. However, they made little progress, for the hole was dug *parallel* to the fence, gradually becoming a trench. Finally, they were assisted by another dog, who dug them out from the other side. True story."

SONDRA AUDIN ARMER notes that of her first five poems published in literary journals, four were about animals. The next fifty to appear were more varied, but creatures great and small populate many pages. She's had furred, feathered, and finned companions throughout her life, including four dogs. She thinks all species must be protected by and from featherless bipeds.

RENEE ASHLEY's collection *Salt* won the Brittingham Prize in Poetry (Univ. of Wisconsin Press, 1991). She comments, "Dogs? A life full of them—stray dogs, pound dogs, all wonderful dogs. Can't imagine my life without them. Wouldn't want to."

JEFF AVANTS lives with his wife and two children in Ventura, California, and works in the book sales trade.

DAVID BAKER is author of four books of poems, most recently *After the Reunion* (Univ. of Arkansas Press, 1994). He teaches at Denison University in Ohio. His family history includes a mother, father, brother, wife, daughter, four dogs, and more than fifteen trillion fleas, ticks, and dog bones.

ANGELA BALL teaches in the Center for Writers, University of Southern Mississippi. Her books of poems include *Kneeling Between Parked Cars* and *Quartet*. She has always wanted a dog.

ROBIN BECKER teaches at Penn State and is a Board Member of the Associated Writing Programs. Her books include *Giacometti's Dog* (Pittsburgh) and *Backtalk* (Alice James Books).

MARCK L. BEGGS, Ph.D., teaches writing at the University of Arkansas at Little Rock and jokes that his current dog, Sloppy Joe, is smarter than any of his students. He writes, "Kilty Sue died in 1989, the victim of a serial poisoner in Denver. Neighbors, look out for your neighbors' pets."

MARVIN BELL lives in Iowa City, Iowa, and Port Townsend, Washington. His thirteen books include *The Book of the Dead Man* (poems) and *A Marvin Bell Reader* (selected poems and prose). In 1994, he received an Award in Literature from the American Academy of Arts and Letters. He explains, "Pythias was the younger brother of Daedalus, a Vermont dog who sat with us evenings when I taught for Goddard College, and who would go home when I said to. Pythias, being younger, was less linguistic. Prince was a Long Island dog."

DAVID BIESPIEL was born in Oklahoma in 1964 and grew up in Texas. He has taught at several universities, most recently at Stanford. The recipient of many awards, he is a contributor to *The New York Times, American Poetry Review*, and other literary magazines.

ELIZABETH BISHOP received the Pulitzer Prize in 1955 for the combined edition of *North & South* and *A Cold Spring. The Complete Poems of Elizabeth Bishop* is published by Farrar, Straus & Giroux.

CATHY SMITH BOWERS has published poems in the *Georgia Review, Poetry*, the *Atlantic*, etc. Her first collection, *The Love that Ended Yesterday in Texas*, was published by Texas Tech. University Press in 1992. She is the winner of a General Electric Award for Younger Writers, a South Poetry Fellowship, and a South Carolina Fiction Project Award. She notes, "the most devastating part of my divorce was losing my dog Seamus Heaney— Mr. Heaney to strangers."

KAY BOYLE, born in St. Paul in 1903, is primarily known as a novelist and short story writer. Her *Collected Poems* was published in 1962.

WILLIAM BRONK has published many books of poetry, the most comprehensive of which is *Life Supports: New and Collected Poems* (North Point). Other collections include *Careless Love, Living Instead*, and *Manifest: and Furthermore*. His collection of essays *Vectors and Smoothable Curves* was also published by North Point. He is considered by many readers of poetry to be among the most important American poets of the second half of the twentieth century.

CHARLES BUKOWSKI is reported to be the most popular American poet outside the borders of the United States. During his lifetime, he published numerous short fiction and poetry collections, including *Burning in Water, Drowning in Flame: Selected Poems 1955–1973* (Black Sparrow Press), where the poem herein previously appeared.

MICHAEL BURKHARD's books include *The Fires They Kept* (Metro Book Co.) and *My Secret Boat* (W. W. Norton).

THOMAS CARPER and his wife, Janet, live in Maine with their present husky mix, Nadia, and a fish, Louis Quatorze. He writes, "Tanya died in 1987, after sixteen years of being first dog in the family, but she lives on in memory and in a handful of poems."

HAYDEN CARRUTH was born in 1921 and for many years lived in northern Vermont. He lives now in upstate New York where until recently he taught in the Graduate Creative Writing Program at Syracuse University. He has published twenty-nine books, chiefly of poetry but including also a novel, four books of criticism, and two anthologies. His most recent books are *Suicides and Jazzers* (1992), *The Collected Shorter Poems* (1992), and *The Collected Longer Poems* (1994). The recipient of numerous awards and grants, he was appointed a Senior Fellow by the NEA in 1988.

RAYMOND CARVER's collections of short fiction include *Will You Please Be Quiet, Please, What We Talk About When We Talk About Love, Cathedral,* and *Where I'm Calling From.* His poetry collections include *Ultramarine, Where Water Comes Together with Other Water,* and *A New Path to the Waterfall.*

SIV CEDERING is a sled that is often pulled on the beaches and roads of East Hampton. She is owned by two magnificent Siberian huskes—Yukon Kalle, who was named after Siv's uncle, who prospected in the Yukon; and Yukon Kalle's daughter, Lappi Borea, who was named after Siv's mother, who was born in Lapland. Siv is presently working on the text, illustrations, and music for six TV programs about a pig, based on her book for children.

MARILYN CHIN is the author of *Dwarf Bamboo* and *The Phoenix Gone, The Terrace Empty* (Milkweed Editions, 1994). She teaches in the MFA Program at San Diego State University. She has won many awards for her poetry, including two NEA Fellowships, a Stegner Fellowship, the Mary Roberts Rinehart Award, and a Pushcart Prize.

DAVID CITINO, Professor of English and Creative Writing at Ohio State University, is currently serving as President of the Board of Trustees of Thurber House. His most recent books are *The Disciple: New & Selected Poems, 1980–1992* (Ohio State) and *The Weight of the Heart* (Quarterly Review of Literature Poetry Series).

ROBIN CLARK, a recent graduate of the MFA Creative Writing Program at Wichita State University, is now working as a technical document specialist in Pittsburgh, Pennsylvania. She believes that all living things deserve respect, and is obsessed with the human link— imagined and real and camouflaged—to nature. When she was a kid she was afraid of dogs.

WILL CLIPMAN is a poet, percussionist, composer, maskmaker, storyteller, and educator from Tucson. His publications include the book *Dog Light* (Wesleyan) and three solo recordings, *Nerve Chorus, Philadelphia,* and *Bone Fire* on the Stillpoint Music label. He serves as an Artist-in-Residence with the Arizona Commission on the Arts and a Performing Artist with Young Audiences, and he performs, records, and tours regionally and nationally with R. Carlos Nakai and Jackalope, the William Eaton Ensemble, and Stefan George & Songtown. "It is a well-known fact that Will's Sonoran coyote hound, Dune, is the best dog in the world," reports Will.

BILLY COLLINS's fifth collection of poetry is *The Art of Drowning* (Univ. of Pittsburgh Press). He is currently without a dog, but is looking for a border collie that will follow him around for the rest of his life.

HENRI COULETTE's *Collected Poems*, edited by Donald Justice, was published in 1992 by the University of Arkansas Press. His poetic career was marked by brilliance and long silences.

MARK COX teaches at Oklahoma State University and for the MFA in Writing Program of Vermont College. The recipient of many grants and awards, he is the author of *Barbells of the God*, *Smoulder*, and *37 Years from the Stone*. He comments, "Dogs, like our good friends, spouses, and children, exist separately from us. They have their own spirits that resist any and all of our projections onto them. They demand that we acknowledge both their individuality and our responsibility for them. And in so doing, they serve as reflectors for our own lives—who we are and how we've become who we are. Long before I became a parent, my dog Beau taught me a lot about how I was raised, how I should grow old, and how I should come to terms with death. In many ways, he was the one who took care of me."

MARY CROW, the author of several collections of poetry, most recently *Borders*, has won a Colorado Book Award for her translations, *Vertical Poetry: Recent Poems of Roberto Juarroz*. She teaches for the Creative Writing Program of Colorado State University.

ROBERT DANA's new book is *Yes, Everything* (Another Chicago Press, 1994). His work was awarded the Delmore Schwartz Memorial Poetry Prize in 1988, and has earned the author two NEA Fellowships for Poetry. He has recently retired after forty years of full-time teaching, but you'd never know it to look at him. He reports himself to be part Skye blue terrier.

JAMES DICKEY notes having once said, in *Self-Interviews*, "Thomas Aquinas, who has a long explanation in one of his innumerable works about why animals have no souls: why only men have souls. This idea has always seemed manifestly unjust to me. I think any living thing ought to be credited with a soul. If one species is, then they all ought to be." In his poem, "The Heaven for Animals," Dickey says, "Having no souls, they have come / Anyway, beyond their knowing. . . ."

WILLIAM DICKEY's books of poetry include *In the Dreaming: Selected Poems*, published by University of Arkansas Press in 1994.

STEPHEN DOBYNS's many books include the novel *Cold Dog Soup* and the poetry collection *Black Dog, Red Dog*, as well as *Cemetary Nights*, *Griffon*, *The Balthus Poems*, and *Heat Death*. He teaches at Syracuse University.

STEPHEN DOWDALL is Vice President of Management Training and Organizational Development for Texas Commerce Bank. He lives in Houston with his wife, Katherine, and says, "There isn't a morning that I don't miss Smythe, who now plays with Mona until we can get there to take them for a run."

JOSEPH DUEMER is coeditor of *Dog Music* and Associate Professor of Humanities at Clarkson University. He is author of *Customs* (Univ. of Georgia Press) and *Static* (Owl Creek Press) and editor of *Poets Reading Stevens*, a special issue of *The Wallace Stevens Journal* for which he also serves as poetry editor. He has won two NEA Creative Writing Fellowships, as well as awards from the Associated Writing Programs and the NEH. He and his wife Carole Mathey share their house with Mingo, Maude, and Weezer—an

Australian shepherd/terrier mix, a bluetick hound, and a French bulldog, respectively, all three dyed-in-the-wool empiricists.

STEPHEN DUNN is the author of nine books of poems, including the recently published *News & Selected Poems: 1974–1994* (W. W. Norton). He teaches at Richard Stockton College in New Jersey.

RUSSELL EDSON writes, "Early on I was bitten by a werewolf, and have loved dogs ever since—even pussycats. . . ."

RON EZZIE lives and writes in Colorado.

LAWRENCE FERLINGHETTI has published numerous poetry collections over the last several decades. The poem herein appeared earlier in *A Coney Island of the Mind*, published by New Directions.

DONALD FINKEL, the author of twelve volumes of poetry and one of translation, was until 1992 Poet-in-Residence at Washington University in St. Louis. He is married to poet and novelist Constance Urdang, and father of Liza, Tom, and Amy. He comments, "Binker, the hound in question, like all the creatures who've shared their lives with us, was a careful student of our culture, a true multiculturalist. It was (and it remains, we believe) up to us all to return the compliment."

CAROL FROST's latest book *Pure*, is from TriQuarterly Books. She is the recipient of two NEA Fellowships in Poetry and directs the Catskill Poetry Workshop at Harwick College, where she is Writer-in-Residence. She reports that her serious association with dogs began when she was seven and responsible for the care and feeding of a birthday puppy. She still wants a springer spaniel.

RICHARD FROST is Professor of English at the State University College, Oneonta, New York. He has published two chapbooks, as well as two full-length collections with Ohio University Press. The recipient of an NEA Fellowship in 1992, he lives in an old farmhouse with his wife Carol Frost and their dog.

REYES GARCIA is the author of *A Philosopher in Aztlan*. He teaches philosphy at Fort Lewis College in Durango, Colorado.

MICHAEL GESSNER, who lives and writes in Cassa Grande, Arizona, had this to say on learning that his poem "Lines on a Dog's Face" was to be published by *Oxford Magazine*: "I informed Cynthia. She was unimpressed. I put some Pedigree canned meat in her evening dish and she was grateful for this—predictably so." Presumably Cynthia will have a similar reaction to her appearance in these pages.

LOUISE GLÜCK lives in Vermont and teaches at Williams College. Her most recent collection, *The Wild Iris* (Ecco, 1992), was awarded the Pulitzer Prize.

ALBERT GOLDBARTH's collection *Heaven and Earth* received the National Book Critics Circle Award; his most recent books are *Marriage, and Other Science Fiction* (poems) and *Great Topics of the World* (essays). Currently dogless, he notes that he was in large part shaped during his formative years by close associations with "the noble Duke and the neurotic Tuffy." Some consider him the most prolific poet in the universe, as well as one of the best.

DAVID GRAHAM is the author of four colletions of poems, most recently *Doggedness* and *Second Wind* (an AWP Award selection). His poems, essays, and reviews have appeared widely. He is Chair of the English Department at Ripon College. His current dog is an English springer spaniel named Spim. He comments, "I wrote my collection *Doggedness* in part to see if I could better understand something of my own long-standing love of dogs, and how it might connect to larger cultural and philosophical issues. If I had to summarize, I would probably quote a remark I heard Galway Kinnell make once: that if the study of ecology means anything at all, it means that we are all cousins on this earth."

THOM GUNN, Anglo-American poet, born in 1929, lives in San Francisco. He possesses no dog, but watches dogs with pleasure. He is the author, most recently, of *The Man with Night Sweats.*

RACHEL HADAS is the author of *Slow Transparency, Pass it On, Mirrors of Astonishment,* and *Other Words than This* (1994), as well as two volumes of literary essays. She was educated at Radcliffe and Johns Hopkins, and lived several years in Greece.

SIDNEY HALL JR. is a publisher, an editor, a Latin teacher, and a conservationist whose poems have appeared in numerous literary journals and in the *Los Angeles Times Book Review.* His collection *What We Will Give Each Other* was published by Hobblebush Books. He writes, "Dogs are not only an important physical presence in my life, but I see them also as inexplicable metaphors. This poem ("Lazy Sleeping Dogs") expresses one possibility."

MICHAEL S. HARPER has taught at Brown University for twenty-five years; he is University Professor and Professor of English, and was first Poet Laureate for the State of Rhode Island, 1988–1993. He has published ten books of poetry and edited four others, including *Every Shut Eye Ain't Asleep: African-American Poetry from 1945 to the Present* (Little Brown, 1994). *Honorable Amendments,* a new book of poems, will be published in 1995 by University of Illinois Press; his *Collected Poems* will be published by Illinois in 1996. He notes, "A gift for my children from grandmother, Sandra was a half setter/half retriever with a sweet disposition, good with children."

WILLIAM HATHAWAY "has run with the dogs under the hounded moon, slept with the dogs in their straw-floored houses, and finally he has gone to the dogs to lick his wounds in the curled warmth of their infinite mercy."

H. L. HIX's most recent book is *Spirit Hovering Over the Ashes: Legacies of Postmodern Theory,* published by SUNY Press. His basset hound is named Katy, but also answers to "Pooper."

LINDA HOGAN is a Chickasaw poet, novelist, and essayist. She is the author of several books of poetry and a collection of short fiction. Her novel *Mean Spirit* (Atheneum) received the Oklahoma Book Award and the Mountains and Plains Booksellers Award. *Seeing Through the Sun* received an American Book Award from the Before Columbus Foundation. *The Book of Medicines* was published in 1993. The recipient of awards, fellowship, and grants from the NEA, the Guggenheim Foundation, and others, she is an Associate Professor at the University of Colorado.

ANSELM HOLLO teaches poetics at the Naropa Institute in Boulder, Colorado. His books include *Outlying Districts* (Coffee House Press), where the poem included here previously appeared.

MIROSLAV HOLUB has been called the most important poet working in Europe today. He has been chief research immunologist at the Institute for Clinical and Experimental Medicine in Prague. His book, *Sagital Section*, translated by Stuart Friebert, is the third volume of the Field Translation Series.

CHRISTOPHER HOWELL's sixth collection of poems, *Memory and Heaven*, will be published in 1996 by Eastern Washington University Press. About his poems included here, he says, "Both concern the same dog, who was with me seventeen years and who frequently caused me to remember that saying attributed to St. Francis to the effect that all creatures are actually or potentially angels. His spirit seemed real, intimate, and responsive, and angelic or not was a welcome argument against the rational materialism that insists we own the planet."

RICHARD JACKSON is the author of three books of poems, most recently *Alive All Day*, and two books of criticism; he has edited an anthology of Slovene poetry. He teaches at the University of Tennessee–Chattanooga where he has won several teaching awards, edits *Poetry Miscellany* and *Mala Revija*, and runs the Meacham Writers' Workshops. A member of PEN's Sarajevo committee, his poems have been published in several languages.

STAN JAMES is a philosopher, sheetmetal worker, and desktop publishing expert; he and his wife Victoria, a teacher, have lived mostly in Washington and California. He writes, "When I was discharged from Viet Nam / and the navy of this country in '72, I spent / six weeks of August and September / on land bound over for clearcut / . . . . My primary camp-mate was Nicholas, / A labrador-setter adolescent, / who was pitiless. We ate, dozed, moved / our bowels, and did our parallel sums. / He hunted ground squirrels in the burn, / I worked on the only decent tan of my life."

DONALD JUSTICE was born in Miami, Florida, and is now living in Iowa City, Iowa. His most recent book is *A Donald Justice Reader* (1991). In 1980, he was awarded the Pulitzer Prize for his *Selected Poems*. He writes, "As for dogs, I have loved them all my life."

RICHARD KATROVAS published his first three books with Wesleyan University Press, and his most recent one, *The Book of Complaints*, with Carnegie Mellon University Press, which will publish his *Dithyrambs* in 1997. His poems, prose fiction, reviews, and essays have appeared widely. He reports that though his dog Spot lives with his ex-wife, he has visiting privileges.

WELDON KEES, born in Nebraska in 1914, was a jazz pianist, a filmmaker, a painter, and a poet who published three collections during his lifetime. The *Collected Poems of Weldon Kees*, edited by Donald Justice, was published by the University of Nebraska Press.

BRIGIT PEGEEN KELLY teaches in the Creative Writing Program at the University of Illinois at Urbana–Champaign. Her second book, *Song*, published by BOA Editions, was the 1994 Lamont Poetry Selection of the Academy of American Poets.

MARY KINZIE is the author of four volumes of poetry, most recently *Autumn Eros* (Knopf).

MAXINE KUMIN was awarded the Pulitzer Prize in 1973. The author of numerous collections of poetry, several novels, a collection of essays on country living, and a collection of short stories, she lives in New Hampshire.

GREG KUZMA writes, "Barb and I had three wonderful dogs—Penny, Spintop, and Starbright. Penny was mother to the others. They lived with us for nearly fifteen years. We have not replaced them. I have written dozens of poems about them."

SYDNEY LEA is the author of five books of poems, a novel, and a recent volume of personal essays entitled *Hunting the Whole Way Home* (Univ. Press of New England). Much of that collection of essays is devoted to working with gundogs, who have led him, Lea says, "into country and into nonverbal modes of communication so beautiful as to remain beyond words, in poetry or otherwise."

DENISE LEVERTOV, born in England, is one of the most widely read and influential poets of the century. She served as a nurse in London during World War II and became an American citizen in 1955. Associated with William Carlos Williams and the Objectivists, her influence has continued to affect subsequent generations of American poets. Her *Selected Poems* was published in 1985.

PHILIP LEVINE was born and educated in Detroit and lives in Fresno, California. Among his many collections are *Not This Pig, They Feed They Lion, The Names of the Lost, Ashes, Sweet Will*, and *A Walk with Tom Jefferson*. He reports, "I once worked as a mailman in Palo Alto, California, and two particular dogs—both in the poem—made life a nightmare. We, these dogs and I, all survived that summer." He adds that he really doesn't "dislike dogs as much as the poem suggests, and in fact the first time the poem was reprinted in an anthology I included an apology to a particular dog, Pumpkin, now gone, but then the mascot of the Grolier Poetry Book Store in Cambridge."

THOMAS LUX has published six collections of poems, the latest of which is *Split Horizon* (Houghton Mifflin, 1994). He teaches at Sarah Lawrence College.

THOMAS McAFEE, born in Alabama in 1928, is the author of numerous collections of short fiction and poetry, including *The Body & the Body's Guest: New & Selected Poems* (BkMk, 1975), and of the novel *Rover Youngblood*. For much of his life, he taught at the University of Missouri–Columbia, where he was beloved by his students.

MARTHA McFERREN has published four books of poetry: *Delusions of a Popular Mind, Get Me Out of Here!, Contours for Ritual*, and *Women in Cars*. She has received fellowships from the Louisiana Arts Council, Yaddo, and the NEA. Her poems have appeared in numerous periodicals and anthologies. She lives in New Orleans.

THOMAS McGRATH's books of poetry include *The Movie at the End of the World: Collected Poems* (Ohio Univ. Press/Swallow Press).

FREYA MANFRED lives in Shorewood, Minnesota, with her husband, Tom Pope, and twin sons. Her latest long poem, *The Madwoman and the Mask*, appears as a video on KTCA (educational) TV. She writes novels and has started a screenplay. Currently residing with two cats, she reports that, now that she has a place for one to play and to walk outside, she is eager to find a dog.

PAUL MARIANI's most recent books are *Salvage Operations: New & Selected Poems* (W. W. Norton, 1990) and *Lost Puritan: A Life of Robert Lowell* (Norton, 1994). A new book of poems, *Shadow Portraits*, will be published in 1995. He writes, "Aren't animals, dogs in particular, like angels sent among us to instruct us on the business of being human?"

WILLIAM MATTHEWS's *Selected Poems and Translations 1969–1991* was published in 1992 by Houghton Mifflin, who also brought out Matthews's *Time & Money* in 1995. A reviewer once said of his work, "I wish Mr. Matthews would curb his enthusiasm for writing about dogs. . . ." Since then, Matthews notes, his works are a kennel, and many a poem, like a Canaletto painting, has one or more dogs in it, not as extras but as accuracies.

JAMES MERRILL, one of America's most distinguished poets, died in 1995. He is the author of many books of poetry, including *The Changing Light at Sandover*, as well as two novels, *Ru Seraglio* and *The (Diplos) Notebook*.

W. S. MERWIN's most recent book of poems is *Travels* (Knopf, 1993). His *The First Four Books* and *The Second Four Books* are published by Copper Canyon. He was the recipient the Dorthea Tanning Prize and the Lenore Marshall Prize in 1994. He writes, "It is hard to talk about any real love. And we have a relationship to dogs that is unique. They exist only because of us. And they have become our teachers."

GILES MITCHELL's collections of poetry include *Love Among the Mad* and *Some Green Laurel*. His scholarly articles have appeared in *American Journal of Psychoanalysis, Psychoanalytic Review*, and *American Imago*. He has an earlier book on the art theme in Joyce Cary's first trilogy. He notes, "For some nice comments on Dogs and Goddesses, see Erlich's *A Match to My Heart*."

MICHAEL MOOS, who lives in St. Paul, Minnesota, with his golden retriever, four cats, and a parakeet, has an MFA from Columbia University. He has published three collections of poetry: *Hawk Hover, Morning Windows*, and *A Long Way to See*. His work has won an NEA Fellowship and a Loft–McKnight Award.

DONALD MORRILL's poems have appeared in journals such as *North American Review, Southern Review*, and *New England Review*. His prose has appeared in *Creative Nonfiction*. He teaches at the University of Tampa and is poetry editor of *Tampa Review*.

LISEL MUELLER's books of poems include *The Private Life*, where the poem herein earlier appeared.

JOAN MURRAY's most recent collection is *The Same Water* (Wesleyan). Her book-length narrative, *Queen of the Mist*, was chosen runner-up for the Poetry Society of America's di Castagnola Award for a manuscript in progress. She spent her childhood terrified of dogs, but is now fully rehabilitated.

JACK MYERS's latest book is *Blindside* (Godine, 1993). He teaches creative writing at Southern Methodist University and for the Vermont College MFA Program. He says that the only dog he ever "owned," Sam, ran away because he lived in an unheated warehouse and next door the bartender fed Sam free hot dogs.

HOWARD NEMEROV won many notable literary awards, including the Levinson Prize from *Poetry* magazine and the Fellowship of the Academy of American Poets. He was formally inducted into the American Academy and Institute of Arts and Letters in 1977 and was for much of his life Edward Mallinckrodt Distinguished University Professor at Washington University in St. Louis. His many books of poems include *The Collected Poems of Howard Nemerov*, published by the University of Chicago Press.

GREG PAPE's recent books include *Storm Patterns* (Univ. of Pittsburgh Press, 1992) and *Sunflower Facing the Sun* (Univ. of Iowa Press, 1992). He teaches at the University of Montana and comments, "Dogs have always been part of the family. We should treat them with the respect due any member of the family."

ROBERT PARHAM's *The Low Fire of Keen Memory* will appear this year from Colonial Press. His work has appeared in *Harvard Magazine, William and Mary Review, Plum Review,* and many other periodicals. He writes, "Bullet, Lucretia's dog, shares his affection with me generously until it is returned in kind. As it is."

MICHAEL PETTIT's books include *Cardinal Points* (Iowa) and *American Light*. He is director of the Mount Holyoke Writers' Conference and reports that his retriever, Boscobel, serves as administrative assistant to dispel anxiety.

MICHAEL PFEIFER lives near St. Louis, Missouri, with his wife, Barbara Eldridge, a fiction writer, and their cat Maggie. His poems have appeared in numerous magazines, including *Laurel Review, Northwest Review, Poet Lore,* and *Seattle Review*. He comments, "As a boy I followed the baying of 'coon dogs through the Missouri woods on autumn nights. The memory appeals to my notion of wildness present in the world. On particular nights we can all hear the old night sounds and feel the risk in being alive. To forget our animal nature makes us less human, less alive, and more dangerous. The animals we share our lives with guard us from this."

STANLEY PLUMLY's last book *Boy on the Step*, was published by Ecco in 1989. He writes, "Gee (short for Gee Que) is the most remarkable brindle bulldog alive. His father is a national champion, so Gee has the genes. My poem actually understates his virtues."

LAWRENCE RAAB is the author of four collections of poetry, most recently *What We Don't Know About Each Other* (Penguin, 1993). He teaches at Williams College. His dog, Katie, was found in an animal shelter in Vermont.

CARL RAKOSI is the last surviving member of the Objectivist poets of the 1930s. His *Collected Poems* was published by the National Poetry Foundation in 1986 and his *Collected*

Prose in 1983. The NPF has also published *Carl Rakosi, Man and Poet*, a book of critical essays about his work. Sun & Moon Press brought out an edition of his very early poems in 1994. His work has been translated into French, German, Italian, Polish, Russian, and Hungarian.

BIN RAMKE is editor of *Denver Quarterly* and of the Contemporary Poetry Series of the University of Georgia Press. He teaches at the University of Denver. He has a cat.

DAVID RAY's poems about New Zealand, *Wool Highway*, won the William Carlos Williams Award. His poems about Australia are collected in *Kangaroo Poems* (Thomas Jefferson University Press, 1994). Next to Albert Goldbarth, he is America's second most prolific poet.

ADRIENNE RICH's many collections include *Diving into the Wreck*, which was co-winner of the 1974 National Book Award, *Your Native Land, Your Life*, and *The Fact of a Doorframe: Poems Selected and New 1950–1984*, published by Norton. In 1993 W. W. Norton also published *What is Found There: Notebooks on Poetry and Politics.*

BOYER RICKEL teaches at the University of Arizona in Tucson. He is the author of *Arreboles* (Univ. Press of New England).

MICHAEL J. ROSEN has published several books relating to dogs and animal welfare since 1990, when he established the Company of Animals Fund, which offers grants to humane organizations across the country via the profits from anthologies that include over one hundred writers and illustrators.

LIZ ROSENBERG's books of poetry include *The Angel Poems* and *The Fire Music* (Univ. of Pittsburgh Press) where her "Elegy for a Beagle Mutt" earlier appeared.

DENNIS SCHMITZ's most recent collection is *About Night: Selected & New Poems* (Field Editions, Oberlin College Press, 1993).

JAMES SEAY teaches at the University of North Carolina at Chapel Hill. His most recent book of poems is *The Light As They Found It*, published by Morrow.

BRENDA SHAW writes, "A New England farm girl, I went on to become a biological research scientist in Scotland, married an Englishman, and have raised two sons, several dogs, and many cats. Now 'retired' and living in Oregon, I write poetry, fiction, and memoirs. A house is not a home without a dog, and I'm a sucker for strays."

CHARLES SIMIC was born in Yugoslavia in 1938 and currently lives in New Hampshire. His many books of poetry have earned praise and recognition in the form of awards, grants, and fellowships from the American Academy of Arts and Letters, the National Institute of Arts and Letters, the Guggenheim Foundation, and the Poetry Society of America. He is a recipient of the Pulitzer Prize.

JIM SIMMERMAN is coeditor of *Dog Music*. His collections of poems include *Home, Once Out of Nature*, and *Moon Go Away, I Don't Love You No More*. An English Professor at Northern Arizona University, he lives in Flagstaff with the Bandit, an all-American mixed breed adopted (not the first) from the local shelter.

MAURYA SIMON has published five volumes of poetry, most recently *The Golden Labyrinth* (Univ. of Missouri Press, 1995). She teaches in the Creative Writing Department at the University of California–Riverside.

WILLIAM STAFFORD (1914–1993) lived a life devoted to peace, conscience, and "purifying the language of the tribe."

FRANK STANFORD was born in Mississippi in 1948. He published eight collections of poetry during his lifetime, including *The Battlefield Where the Moon Says I Love You*, a 542-page poem. Several collections of his poetry and prose have appeared since his death in 1978 and more publications are anticipated.

GERALD STERN's two most recent books are *Selected Poems* (Harper) and *Bread Without Sugar* (W. W. Norton). *Odd Mercy* will be published in 1995 by W. W. Norton.

FRANK STEWART has published three books of poems and is a winner of the Whiting Writers Award. His most recent book is *A Natural History of Nature Writing* (Island Press, 1995), which traces, in part, the development of America's ethical awareness of the natural world.

PAMELA STEWART, whose fourth book *Infrequent Mysteries* was published by Alice James Books, lives on a small farm in western Massachusetts. She writes, "Both the routines and surprises of caring for our three dogs (and some sixteen other creatures) is pure nourishment to me. It is one way I can be sure of doing good in this world, of returning the favor of being alive."

ROBERT SWARD is a longtime dog lover. His first book, *Uncle Dog & Other Poems*, was published in England. His twelfth and most recent book is *Four Incarnations, New & Selected Poems* (Coffee House Press, 1991). Winner of a Guggenheim Fellowship and a Villa Montalvo Literary Arts Award, he teaches for the University of California Extension in Santa Cruz.

SUNTARO TANIKAWA is a Japanese poet of note, whose work has achieved a presence in the English language via the graceful translations of Harold Wright.

ELIZABETH MARSHALL THOMAS is the author of *The Hidden Life of Dogs, The Tribe of Tiger: Cats and their Culture, The Animal Wife, Reindeer Moon*, both novels, and other books. She is currently at work, she reports, on a book about living in groups of mixed species—people, dogs, and cats. She has spent many years studying animals, and now writes about them.

JOHN UPDIKE was born in Pennsylvania in 1932 and was, from 1955–1957, a member of the staff of *The New Yorker*. He is the author of numerous poems, short stories, essays, book reviews, and novels. His fiction has won the Pulitzer Prize, the National Book Award, the American Book Award, and the National Book Critics Circle Award. His *Collected Poems* was published by Knopf in 1993.

GLORIA VANDO's collection of poems *Promesas: Geography of the Impossible* (Arte Publico Press, 1993) won the 1993 Thorpe Menn Book Award. Her poems have appeared in *Western Humanities Review, Kenyon Review, Cottonwood, Seattle Review*, etc., and in numerous anthologies, most recently *In Other Words: Literature by Latinas of the United States*. She is founder and publisher of Helicon Nine Editions in Kansas City, where she watches birds, foxes, raccoons, deer, and lots of dogs.

ELLEN BRYANT VOIGT has published four volumes of poetry, most recently *Two Trees*. Her fifth book, *Kyrie*, is forthcoming from W. W. Norton in 1995. She founded and directed the low-residency MFA Writing Program at Goddard College and teaches at its relocated incarnation at Warren Wilson College in Swannanoa, North Carolina. The recipient of fellowships from the NEA, the Guggenheim Foundation, and the Lila Wallace foundation, she lives in Cabot, Vermont, with her husband and two children.

NANCY B. WALL lives and writes in Tucson, Arizona.

MICHAEL WATERS has published five volumes of poetry, including *Bountiful* (1992), *The Burden Lifters* (1989), and *Anniversary of the Air* (1985)—these titles from Carnegie Mellon. The recipient of a fellowship from the NEA, two Individual Artist Awards from the Maryland State Arts Council, and two Pushcart Prizes, he teaches at Salisbury State University on the Eastern Shore of Maryland.

BRUCE WEIGL "has known and loved some good dogs." His most recent book, from TriQuarterly Books, is *What Saves Us.*

JAMES WELCH's first book of poems, *Riding the Earthboy 40*, was also his last, though he has gone on to publish a number of critically acclaimed novels, including *The Indian Lawyer* and *Fools Crow*.

WARREN WIGUTOW lives in Norwood, New York, and has been a committed ethical vegetarian for twenty-five years. He currently lives "in a dogless house which is still mourning its loss last year of Sitwell, a wise setter/Lab pound refugee."

RICHARD WILBUR, essayist, translator, and poet, has won both the Pulitzer Prize and the National Book Award. Among his many poetry collections is *Ceremony and Other Poems*, where his poem herein previously appeared.

C. K. WILLIAMS lives in Paris, but spends part of each year teaching at George Mason University. His most recent collections of poetry are *Poems 1963–1983*, *Flesh and Blood*, and *A Dream of Mind*, as well as an influential translation of Euripides' *The Bacchae*.

WILLIAM CARLOS WILLIAMS, one of the greatest American poets of the twentieth century, is the author of numerous collections, including *Pictures from Brueghel and Other Poems* (New Directions), which was awarded the Pulitzer Prize in 1963. He is the subject of a biography by Paul Mariani, another contributor to *Dog Music*.

KEITH WILSON is a New Mexican poet and short story writer whose most recent work is *Graves Registry* (Clark City Press, 1992). He writes, "Dogs have been my spiritual advisors throughout my life. No fooling."

CHARLES WRIGHT is the author of *Country Music* and *The World of the Ten Thousand Things*, along with many other books. He lives in Charlottesville, Virginia.

JAMES WRIGHT was born in Martins Ferry, Ohio, in 1927. His *Collected Poems* won the 1972 Pulitzer Prize for poetry. He died in 1980. *Above the River: the Complete Poems*, a Wesleyan Edition, was published by Farrar, Straus & Giroux and University Press of New England in 1990.

PAUL ZIMMER's books of poetry include *Family Reunion: Selection and New Poems* (Univ. of Pittsburgh Press, 1983) and *Big Blue Train* (Univ. of Arkansas Press, 1993).

TOTALLY BLACKED OUT™

Shakespeare BLACKOUT GAMES™

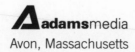

Adamsmedia

Avon, Massachusetts

Copyright © 2012 by F+W Media, Inc.
All rights reserved.
This book, or parts thereof, may not be reproduced in any
form without permission from the publisher; exceptions are
made for brief excerpts used in published reviews.

Published by
Adams Media, a division of F+W Media, Inc.
57 Littlefield Street, Avon, MA 02322. U.S.A.
www.adamsmedia.com

Totally Blacked Out and Blackout Games are trademarks of
Adams Media, a division of F+W Media, Inc.

ISBN 10: 1-4405-3278-8
ISBN 13: 978-1-4405-3278-8

Printed in the United States of America.

10   9   8   7   6   5   4   3   2   1

This publication is designed to provide accurate and authoritative information
with regard to the subject matter covered. It is sold with the understanding
that the publisher is not engaged in rendering legal, accounting, or other
professional advice. If legal advice or other expert assistance is required, the
services of a competent professional person should be sought.
—From a *Declaration of Principles* jointly adopted by a Committee of the
American Bar Association and a Committee of Publishers and Associations

Many of the designations used by manufacturers and sellers to distinguish
their product are claimed as trademarks. Where those designations appear in
this book and Adams Media was aware of a trademark claim, the designations
have been printed with initial capital letters.

This book is available at quantity discounts for bulk purchases.
For information, please call 1-800-289-0963.

Contents

Introduction

Finally—a word game that *encourages* you to scribble outside the lines! Combining the simplicity of word search with the creativity of magnetic poetry, *Shakespeare Blackout Games™* blows those boring, been-there-done-that puzzles out of the water.

Taking gaming to next level, this book inspires you to think outside the puzzle and look at your favorite (or least favorite) works from William Shakespeare with a new perspective. Through blacking out words and phrases, you can transform classic pieces of literature into outrageous, poetic, or truly bizarre messages. You'll feel like a kid again as you black out words in the shape of a heart in a passage from *Romeo and Juliet* or create a fortune cookie message with words plucked ~~struck~~ from *Merchant of Venice*. With *Shakespeare Blackout Games™*, you'll absolutely love rewriting Shakespeare's most famous stories and sonnets—one blacked-out word at a time!

HOW TO USE THIS BOOK

Inside this book, you'll find more than 100 puzzles to complete. Each chapter includes detailed directions and a completed example to inspire you. You'll create original messages by blacking out unused words with a marker, but be careful—once they're hidden behind that layer of ink, they're gone forever!

Here's how you get started:

1. Grab a marker or pen; the darker the better.
2. Read the passage carefully and think about what messages can be created out of your favorite words.
3. Make a small mark identifying each word you want to use in your poem (unless you have an awesome memory).
4. ~~Cross~~ black out everything else.
5. When you're done, your message will read like a complete (and perhaps incredibly poetic!) thought.

NOTE:

To prevent your genius from bleeding through the pages, please place a piece of paper or card stock behind the page before you begin your Totally Blacked Out™ fun.

CHAPTER ONE

Literature's Alphabet

We're starting with the basics for this first chapter: the alphabet. Sure, it sounds like a breeze, but you've really never seen the alphabet quite like this before. In the following puzzles, you'll have to create a message only using words that begin with the letters assigned to that puzzle, so make sure to pay close attention. If you get stuck, try starting your message at the bottom of the page or in the middle of the passage, and remember that you don't always have to use the words in the order that they appear. You may also find it helpful to also search *within* words to help complete your message.

Create a message using words that begin with consonants.

Macbeth (Act II, Scene ii)

Message: the house shall sleep no more when they wash his blood

Create a message using words that begin with the letters "A," "B," "C," and "D."

When I do count the clock that tells the time,
And see the brave day sunk in hideous night;
When I behold the violet past prime,
And sable curls, all silvered o'er with white;
When lofty trees I see barren of leaves,
Which erst from heat did canopy the herd,
And summer's green all girded up in sheaves,
Borne on the bier with white and bristly beard,
Then of thy beauty do I question make,
That thou among the wastes of time must go,
Since sweets and beauties do themselves forsake
And die as fast as they see others grow;
And nothing 'gainst Time's scythe can make
    defence
Save breed, to brave him when he takes thee
    hence.

"Sonnet XII"

Create a message using words that begin with consonants.

When midnight comes, knock at my chamber
    window;
I'll order take my mother shall not hear.
Now will I charge you in the band of truth,
When you have conquer'd my yet maiden bed,
Remain there but an hour, nor speak to me:
My reasons are most strong; and you shall know
    them
When back again this ring shall be deliver'd.
And on your finger in the night I'll put
Another ring, that what in time proceeds
May token to the future our past deeds.
Adieu till then; then fail not. You have won
A wife of me, though there my hope be done.

All's Well That Ends Well (Act IV, Scene ii)

Create a message using words that begin with the letters "E," "F," "G," and "H."

They brought one Pinch, a hungry lean-fac'd
  villain,
A mere anatomy, a mountebank,
A threadbare juggler, and a fortune-teller,
A needy, hollow-ey'd, sharp-looking wretch,
A living dead man. This pernicious slave,
Forsooth, took on him as a conjurer,
And gazing in mine eyes, feeling my pulse,
And with no face, as 'twere, outfacing me,
Cries out I was possess'd. Then all together
They fell upon me, bound me, bore me thence,
And in a dark and dankish vault at home
There left me and my man, both bound together;
Till, gnawing with my teeth my bonds in sunder,
I gain'd my freedom, and immediately
Ran hither to your Grace; whom I beseech
To give me ample satisfaction
For these deep shames and great indignities.

Comedy of Errors (Act V, Scene i)

13

Create a message using words that begin with consonants.

O thou, my lovely boy, who in thy power
Dost hold Time's fickle glass, his fickle hour;
Who hast by waning grown, and therein show'st
Thy lovers withering, as thy sweet self grow'st.
If Nature, sovereign mistress over wrack,
As thou goest onwards, still will pluck thee
   back,
She keeps thee to this purpose, that her skill
May time disgrace and wretched minutes kill.
Yet fear her, O thou minion of her pleasure!
She may detain, but not still keep, her
   treasure:
Her audit (though delayed) answered must be,
And her quietus is to render thee.

"Sonnet CXXVI"

**Create a message using words that begin with the letters
"I," "J," "K," and "L."**

You are too indulgent. Let's grant it is not

Amiss to tumble on the bed of Ptolemy,

To give a kingdom for a mirth, to sit

And keep the turn of tippling with a slave,

To reel the streets at noon, and stand the buffet

With knaves that smell of sweat. Say this
   becomes him—

As his composure must be rare indeed

Whom these things cannot blemish—yet must
   Antony

No way excuse his foils when we do bear

So great weight in his lightness. If he fill'd

His vacancy with his voluptuousness,

Full surfeits and the dryness of his bones

Call on him for't! But to confound such time

That drums him from his sport and speaks as loud

As his own state and ours—'tis to be chid

As we rate boys who, being mature in knowledge,

Pawn their experience to their present pleasure,

And so rebel to judgment.

Antony and Cleopatra (Act I, Scene iv)

**Create a message using words that begin with the letters
"M," "N," "O," and "P."**

O! how thy worth with manners may I sing,

When thou art all the better part of me?

What can mine own praise to mine own self
  bring?

And what is't but mine own when I praise thee?

Even for this, let us divided live,

And our dear love lose name of single one,

That by this separation I may give

That due to thee which thou deserv'st alone.

O absence! what a torment wouldst thou prove,

Were it not thy sour leisure gave sweet leave,

To entertain the time with thoughts of love,

Which time and thoughts so sweetly doth
  deceive,

And that thou teachest how to make one twain,

By praising him here who doth hence remain.

"Sonnet XXXIX"

Create a message using words that begin with consonants.

This deed unshapes me quite, makes me unpregnant
And dull to all proceedings. A deflow'red maid!
And by an eminent body that enforc'd
The law against it! But that her tender shame
Will not proclaim against her maiden loss,
How might she tongue me! Yet reason dares her
   no;
For my authority bears a so credent bulk
That no particular scandal once can touch
But it confounds the breather. He should have
   liv'd,
Save that his riotous youth, with dangerous
   sense,
Might in the times to come have ta'en revenge,
By so receiving a dishonour'd life
With ransom of such shame. Would yet he had
   liv'd!
Alack, when once our grace we have forgot,
Nothing goes right; we would, and we would not.

Measure for Measure (Act III, Scene iv)

CHAPTER TWO

Few and Far Between

Let's find out how much you really love the stories you've heard since you were little. To solve the puzzles in this chapter, you'll need to black out the least amount of words possible. With several world renowned passages in front of you, it may not seem like a hard task to create your very own poem, but the difficulty here lies in creating an *original* message that sounds more like you than straight from the pages of these beloved stories. Once you're feeling a little creative, take a look at the example we've done and get ready to pen your very own classic tale.

There is a ███ character in ██ life
That to th' observer doth
unfold █Thyself and
thine own ███ waste
thy virtues they
doth ███ torch ,
light them for themselves; for
us
As if we had them not.

Measure for Measure (Act I, Scene i)

Message: There is a character in life That to th' observer doth unfold Thyself and thine own waste/thy virtues they doth torch, light them for themselves; for us, As if we had them not.

My mistress with a monster is in love.
Near to her close and consecrated bower,
While she was in her dull and sleeping hour,
A crew of patches, rude mechanicals,
That work for bread upon Athenian stalls,
Were met together to rehearse a play
Intended for great Theseus' nuptial day.
The shallowest thickskin of that barren sort,
Who Pyramus presented, in their sport
Forsook his scene and ent'red in a brake;
When I did him at this advantage take,
An ass's nole I fixed on his head . . .
I led them on in this distracted fear,
And left sweet Pyramus translated there;
When in that moment, so it came to pass,
Titania wak'd, and straightway lov'd an ass.

Midsummer-Night's Dream (Act III, Scene ii)

From fairest creatures we desire increase,
That thereby beauty's rose might never die,
But as the riper should by time decease,
His tender heir might bear his memory:
But thou contracted to thine own bright eyes,
Feed'st thy light's flame with self-substantial
    fuel,
Making a famine where abundance lies,
Thy self thy foe, to thy sweet self too cruel:
Thou that art now the world's fresh ornament,
And only herald to the gaudy spring,
Within thine own bud buriest thy content,
And tender churl mak'st waste in niggarding:
Pity the world, or else this glutton be,
.To eat the world's due, by the grave and thee.

"Sonnet I"

If music be the food of love, play on,
Give me excess of it, that, surfeiting,
The appetite may sicken and so die.
That strain again! It had a dying fall;
O, it came o'er my ear like the sweet sound
That breathes upon a bank of violets,
Stealing and giving odour! Enough, no more;
'Tis not so sweet now as it was before.
O spirit of love, how quick and fresh art thou!
That, notwithstanding thy capacity
Receiveth as the sea, nought enters there,
Of what validity and pitch soe'er,
But falls into abatement and low price
Even in a minute. So full of shapes is fancy,
That it alone is high fantastical.

Twelfth Night; Or, What You Will (Act I, Scene i)

Who will believe my verse in time to come,
If it were fill'd with your most high deserts?
Though yet heaven knows it is but as a tomb
Which hides your life, and shows not half your
    parts.
If I could write the beauty of your eyes,
And in fresh numbers number all your graces,
The age to come would say 'This poet lies;
Such heavenly touches ne'er touch'd earthly
    faces.'
So should my papers, yellow'd with their age,
Be scorn'd, like old men of less truth than
    tongue,
And your true rights be term'd a poet's rage
And stretched metre of an antique song:
But were some child of yours alive that time,
You should live twice,—in it, and in my rhyme.

"Sonnet XVII"

Was it the proud full sail of his great verse,
Bound for the prize of all too precious you,
That did my ripe thoughts in my brain inhearse,
Making their tomb the womb wherein they grew?
Was it his spirit, by spirits taught to write,
Above a mortal pitch, that struck me dead?
No, neither he, nor his compeers by night
Giving him aid, my verse astonished.
He, nor that affable familiar ghost
Which nightly gulls him with intelligence,
As victors of my silence cannot boast;
I was not sick of any fear from thence:
But when your countenance fill'd up his line,
Then lacked I matter; that enfeebled mine.

"Sonnet LXXXVI"

Good reasons must of force give place to better.
The people 'twixt Philippi and this ground
Do stand but in a forced affection,
For they have grudged us contribution . . .
Under your pardon. You must note beside
That we have tried the utmost of our friends,
Our legions are brim-full, our cause is ripe:
The enemy increaseth every day;
We, at the height, are ready to decline.
There is a tide in the affairs of men
Which taken at the flood leads on to fortune;
Omitted, all the voyage of their life
Is bound in shallows and in miseries.
On such a full sea are we now afloat,
And we must take the current when it serves,
Or lose our ventures.

Julius Ceasar (Act IV, Scene ii)

To be, or not to be—that is the question:
Whether 'tis nobler in the mind to suffer
The slings and arrows of outrageous fortune
Or to take arms against a sea of troubles,
And by opposing end them. To die—to sleep—
No more; and by a sleep to say we end
The heartache, and the thousand natural shocks
That flesh is heir to. 'Tis a consummation
Devoutly to be wish'd. To die—to sleep.
To sleep—perchance to dream: ay, there's the
    rub!
For in that sleep of death what dreams may come
When we have shuffled off this mortal coil,
Must give us pause. There's the respect
That makes calamity of so long life.
For who would bear the whips and scorns of
    time . . .
When he himself might his quietus make
With a bare bodkin?

Hamlet, Prince of Denmark (Act III, Scene i)

Thou, Nature, art my goddess; to thy law
My services are bound. Wherefore should I
Stand in the plague of custom, and permit
The curiosity of nations to deprive me,
For that I am some twelve or fourteen moonshines
Lag of a brother? Why bastard? wherefore base?
When my dimensions are as well compact,
My mind as generous, and my shape as true,
As honest madam's issue? Why brand they us
With base? with baseness? bastardy? base, base?
. . . Legitimate Edgar, I must have your land.
Our father's love is to the bastard Edmund
As to th' legitimate. Fine word- 'legitimate'!
Well, my legitimate, if this letter speed,
And my invention thrive, Edmund the base
Shall top th' legitimate. I grow; I prosper.
Now, gods, stand up for bastards!

King Lear (Act I, Scene ii)

No, faith, die by attorney. The poor world is almost six thousand years old, and in all this time there was not any man died in his own person, videlicet, in a love-cause. Troilus had his brains dash'd out with a Grecian club; yet he did what he could to die before, and he is one of the patterns of love. Leander, he would have liv'd many a fair year, though Hero had turn'd nun, if it had not been for a hot midsummer night; for, good youth, he went but forth to wash him in the Hellespont, and, being taken with the cramp, was drown'd; and the foolish chroniclers of that age found it was—Hero of Sestos. But these are all lies: men have died from time to time, and worms have eaten them, but not for love.

As You Like It (Act IV, Scene i)

That such a crafty devil as is his mother
Should yield the world this ass! A woman that
Bears all down with her brain; and this her son
Cannot take two from twenty, for his heart,
And leave eighteen. Alas, poor princess,
Thou divine Imogen, what thou endur'st,
Betwixt a father by thy step-dame govern'd,
A mother hourly coining plots, a wooer
More hateful than the foul expulsion is
Of thy dear husband, than that horrid act
Of the divorce he'd make! The heavens hold firm
The walls of thy dear honour, keep unshak'd
That temple, thy fair mind, that thou mayst
    stand
T' enjoy thy banish'd lord and this great land!

Cymbeline (Act II, Scene i)

How heavy do I journey on the way,
When what I seek, my weary travel's end,
Doth teach that ease and that repose to say,
'Thus far the miles are measured from thy
   friend!'
The beast that bears me, tired with my woe,
Plods dully on, to bear that weight in me,
As if by some instinct the wretch did know
His rider lov'd not speed, being made from thee:
The bloody spur cannot provoke him on,
That sometimes anger thrusts into his hide,
Which heavily he answers with a groan,
More sharp to me than spurring to his side;
For that same groan doth put this in my mind,
My grief lies onward, and my joy behind.

"Sonnet L"

The Greatest Expectation

Time for a ~~little~~ lot of fun! In this chapter, we're giving you full permission to wreak havoc on all your favorite (or most loathed) stories. That's right, in order to finish the following puzzles, you'll need to create a message by blacking out as many words as possible. Just remember that you should still be left with a complete thought at the end of each ink-filled puzzle. If you're looking for more of a challenge, try to beat our sample puzzle or test your blackout skills against your friends!

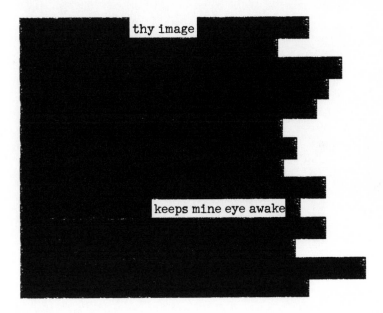

thy image

keeps mine eye awake

"Sonnet LXI"

Message: thy image keeps mine eye awake

47

Since I left you, mine eye is in my mind;
And that which governs me to go about
Doth part his function and is partly blind,
Seems seeing, but effectually is out;
For it no form delivers to the heart
Of bird, of flower, or shape which it doth latch:
Of his quick objects hath the mind no part,
Nor his own vision holds what it doth catch;
For if it see the rud'st or gentlest sight,
The most sweet favour or deformed'st creature,
The mountain or the sea, the day or night:
The crow, or dove, it shapes them to your feature.
Incapable of more, replete with you,
My most true mind thus maketh mine untrue.

If it were done when 'tis done, then 'twere well
It were done quickly. If the assassination
Could trammel up the consequence, and catch,
With his surcease, success; that but this blow
Might be the be-all and the end-all -here,
But here, upon this bank and shoal of time,
We'll jump the life to come. But in these cases
We still have judgement here, that we but teach
Bloody instructions, which being taught return
To plague the inventor. This even-handed
    justice
Commends the ingredients of our poison'd
    chalice
To our own lips . . .
I have no spur
To prick the sides of my intent, but only
Vaulting ambition, which o'erleaps itself
And falls on the other.

Macbeth (Act I, Scene vii)

As fast as thou shalt wane, so fast thou grow'st,
In one of thine, from that which thou
  departest;
And that fresh blood which youngly thou
  bestow'st,
Thou mayst call thine when thou from youth
  convertest,
Herein lives wisdom, beauty, and increase;
Without this folly, age, and cold decay:
If all were minded so, the times should cease
And threescore year would make the world away.
Let those whom nature hath not made for store,
Harsh, featureless, and rude, barrenly perish:
Look, whom she best endow'd, she gave thee more;
Which bounteous gift thou shouldst in bounty
  cherish:
She carv'd thee for her seal, and meant thereby,
Thou shouldst print more, not let that copy die.

"Sonnet XI"

Marry, so I mean, sweet Katherine, in thy bed.
And therefore, setting all this chat aside,
Thus in plain terms: your father hath consented
That you shall be my wife your dowry greed on;
And will you, nill you, I will marry you.
Now, Kate, I am a husband for your turn;
For, by this light, whereby I see thy beauty,
Thy beauty that doth make me like thee well,
Thou must be married to no man but me;
For I am he am born to tame you, Kate,
And bring you from a wild Kate to a Kate
Conformable as other household Kates.
Here comes your father. Never make denial;
I must and will have Katherine to my wife.

Taming of the Shrew (Act II, Scene i)

Ah, dear Juliet,
Why art thou yet so fair? Shall I believe
That unsubstantial Death is amorous,
And that the lean abhorred monster keeps
Thee here in dark to be his paramour?
For fear of that I still will stay with thee
And never from this palace of dim night
Depart again. Here, here will I remain
With worms that are thy chambermaids . . .
Eyes, look your last!
Arms, take your last embrace! and, lips, O you
The doors of breath, seal with a righteous kiss
A dateless bargain to engrossing death!
Come, bitter conduct; come, unsavoury guide!
Thou desperate pilot, now at once run on
The dashing rocks thy seasick weary bark!
Here's to my love! (Drinks.) O true apothecary!
Thy drugs are quick. Thus with a kiss I die.

Romeo and Juliet (Act V, Scene iii)

No more be griev'd at that which thou hast done:
Roses have thorns, and silver fountains mud:
Clouds and eclipses stain both moon and sun,
And loathsome canker lives in sweetest bud.
All men make faults, and even I in this,
Authorizing thy trespass with compare,
Myself corrupting, salving thy amiss,
Excusing thy sins more than thy sins are;
For to thy sensual fault I bring in sense,—
Thy adverse party is thy advocate,—
And 'gainst myself a lawful plea commence:
Such civil war is in my love and hate,
That I an accessary needs must be,
To that sweet thief which sourly robs from me.

"Sonnet XXXV"

I never saw that you did painting need,
And therefore to your fair no painting set;
I found, or thought I found, you did exceed
That barren tender of a poet's debt:
And therefore have I slept in your report,
That you yourself, being extant, well might show
How far a modern quill doth come too short,
Speaking of worth, what worth in you doth grow.
This silence for my sin you did impute,
Which shall be most my glory being dumb;
For I impair not beauty being mute,
When others would give life, and bring a tomb.
There lives more life in one of your fair eyes
Than both your poets can in praise devise.

"Sonnet LXXXIII"

CHAPTER FOUR

A Different Point of View

We're turning everything upside down with this chapter. Just like before, you'll need to black out words to create a message, but this time, you'll need to construct a sentence that can be read from the bottom of the page to the top of the page. Still can't wrap your head around this new outlook? Use our blackout example for ideas on how to start creating your message. You're sure to have a great time starting at the bottom with these topsy-turvy puzzles!

Hamlet, Prince of Denmark (Act I, Scene ii)

Message: my heart cannot want A weary self

In Belmont is a lady richly left,
And she is fair and, fairer than that word,
Of wondrous virtues. Sometimes from her eyes
I did receive fair speechless messages.
Her name is Portia—nothing undervalu'd
To Cato's daughter, Brutus' Portia.
Nor is the wide world ignorant of her worth;
For the four winds blow in from every coast
Renowned suitors, and her sunny locks
Hang on her temples like a golden fleece,
Which makes her seat of Belmont Colchos' strond,
And many Jasons come in quest of her.
O my Antonio, had I but the means
To hold a rival place with one of them,
I have a mind presages me such thrift
That I should questionless be fortunate.

Merchant of Venice (Act I, Scene i)

I am not Adriana, nor thy wife.

The time was once when thou unurg'd wouldst vow

That never words were music to thine ear,

That never object pleasing in thine eye,

That never touch well welcome to thy hand,

That never meat sweet-savour'd in thy taste,

Unless I spake, or look'd, or touch'd, or carv'd
to thee.

How comes it now, my husband, O, how comes it,

That thou art then estranged from thyself?

Thyself I call it, being strange to me,

That, undividable, incorporate,

Am better than thy dear self's better part.

Ah, do not tear away thyself from me;

For know, my love, as easy mayst thou fall

A drop of water in the breaking gulf,

And take unmingled thence that drop again

Without addition or diminishing,

As take from me thyself, and not me too.

Comedy of Errors (Act II, Scene ii)

Sometimes we see a cloud that's dragonish;
A vapour sometime like a bear or lion,
A tower'd citadel, a pendent rock,
A forked mountain, or blue promontory
With trees upon't that nod unto the world
And mock our eyes with air. Thou hast seen
   these signs;
They are black vesper's pageants . . .
My good knave Eros, now thy captain is
Even such a body. Here I am Antony;
Yet cannot hold this visible shape, my knave.
I made these wars for Egypt; and the Queen—
   Whose heart I thought I had, for she had mine,
Which, whilst it was mine, had annex'd unto't
A million moe, now lost—she, Eros, has
Pack'd cards with Caesar, and false-play'd my
   glory
Unto an enemy's triumph.
Nay, weep not, gentle Eros; there is left us
Ourselves to end ourselves.

Antony and Cleopatra (Act IV, Scene xv)

That time of year thou mayst in me behold

When yellow leaves, or none, or few, do hang

Upon those boughs which shake against the cold,

Bare ruin'd choirs, where late the sweet birds
  sang.

In me thou see'st the twilight of such day

As after sunset fadeth in the west;

Which by and by black night doth take away,

Death's second self, that seals up all in rest.

In me thou see'st the glowing of such fire,

That on the ashes of his youth doth lie,

As the death-bed, whereon it must expire,

Consum'd with that which it was nourish'd by.

This thou perceiv'st, which makes thy love more
  strong,

To love that well, which thou must leave ere
  long.

"Sonnet LXXIII"

Those hours, that with gentle work did frame
The lovely gaze where every eye doth dwell,
Will play the tyrants to the very same
And that unfair which fairly doth excel;
For never-resting time leads summer on
To hideous winter, and confounds him there;
Sap checked with frost, and lusty leaves quite
  gone,
Beauty o'er-snowed and bareness every where:
Then were not summer's distillation left,
A liquid prisoner pent in walls of glass,
Beauty's effect with beauty were bereft,
Nor it, nor no remembrance what it was:
But flowers distill'd, though they with winter
  meet,
Leese but their show; their substance still
  lives sweet.

"Sonnet V"

Music, awake her: strike. (Music)

'Tis time; descend; be stone no more; approach;

Strike all that look upon with marvel. Come;

I'll fill your grave up. Stir; nay, come away.

Bequeath to death your numbness, for from him

Dear life redeems you. You perceive she stirs.

(HERMIONE comes down from the pedestal)

Start not; her actions shall be holy as

You hear my spell is lawful. Do not shun her

Until you see her die again; for then

You kill her double. Nay, present your hand.

When she was young you woo'd her; now in age

Is she become the suitor?

... it appears she lives

Though yet she speak not. Mark a little while.

Please you to interpose, fair madam. Kneel,

And pray your mother's blessing. Turn, good
   lady;

Our Perdita is found.

Winter's Tale (Act V, Scene iii)

Soft you; a word or two before you go.

I have done the state some service, and they
know't.

No more of that. I pray you, in your letters,

When you shall these unlucky deeds relate,

Speak of me as I am; nothing extenuate,

Nor set down aught in malice. Then must you speak

Of one that loved not wisely but too well;

Of one not easily jealous, but, being wrought,

Perplex'd in the extreme; of one whose hand,

Like the base Indian, threw a pearl away

Richer than all his tribe; of one whose subdued
eyes,

Albeit unused to the melting mood,

Drop tears as fast as the Arabian trees

Their medicinal gum. Set you down this;

And say besides, that in Aleppo once,

Where a malignant and a turban'd Turk

Beat a Venetian and traduced the state,

I took by the throat the circumcised dog

And smote him, thus.

Othello, the Moor of Venice (Act V, Scene ii)

Friends, Romans, countrymen, lend me your ears!
I come to bury Caesar, not to praise him . . .
He was my friend, faithful and just to me;
But Brutus says he was ambitious,
And Brutus is an honorable man.
He hath brought many captives home to Rome,
Whose ransoms did the general coffers fill.
Did this in Caesar seem ambitious?
When that the poor have cried, Caesar hath wept;
Ambition should be made of sterner stuff:
Yet Brutus says he was ambitious,
And Brutus is an honorable man.
. . . I speak not to disprove what Brutus spoke,
But here I am to speak what I do know.
You all did love him once, not without cause;
What cause withholds you then to mourn for him?
O judgement, thou art fled to brutish beasts,
And men have lost their reason. Bear with me;
My heart is in the coffin there with Caesar,
And I must pause till it come back to me.

Julius Ceasar (Act III, Scene ii)

They that have power to hurt, and will do none,
That do not do the thing they most do show,
Who, moving others, are themselves as stone,
Unmoved, cold, and to temptation slow;
They rightly do inherit heaven's graces,
And husband nature's riches from expense;
They are the lords and owners of their faces,
Others, but stewards of their excellence.
The summer's flower is to the summer sweet,
Though to itself, it only live and die,
But if that flower with base infection meet,
The basest weed outbraves his dignity:
For sweetest things turn sourest by their deeds;
Lilies that fester, smell far worse than weeds.

"Sonnet XCIV"

$\mathfrak{Switching}$ $\mathfrak{Perspective}$

Think you've mastered flipping around messages? Think again. Like the previous chapter, you'll need to visualize the passages a little differently to solve the following puzzles. However, instead of creating a sentence that can be read from the bottom to the top of the page like before, this time you'll have to make the message read from the right side of the page to left side. Not sure where to start? Glance at our sample for inspiration.

Merchant of Venice (Act V, Scene i)

Message: you must part with your faith to leave a world unkind

83

O! how I faint when I of you do write,
Knowing a better spirit doth use your name,
And in the praise thereof spends all his might,
To make me tongue-tied speaking of your fame!
But since your worth—wide as the ocean is,—
The humble as the proudest sail doth bear,
My saucy bark, inferior far to his,
On your broad main doth wilfully appear.
Your shallowest help will hold me up afloat,
Whilst he upon your soundless deep doth ride;
Or, being wrack'd, I am a worthless boat,
He of tall building, and of goodly pride:
Then if he thrive and I be cast away,
The worst was this,—my love was my decay.

"Sonnet LXXX"

She, Claudio, that you wrong'd, look you restore.

Joy to you, Mariana! Love her, Angelo;

I have confess'd her, and I know her virtue.

Thanks, good friend Escalus, for thy much
    goodness;

There's more behind that is more gratulate.

Thanks, Provost, for thy care and secrecy;

We shall employ thee in a worthier place.

Forgive him, Angelo, that brought you home

The head of Ragozine for Claudio's:

Th' offence pardons itself. Dear Isabel,

I have a motion much imports your good;

Whereto if you'll a willing ear incline,

What's mine is yours, and what is yours is mine.

So, bring us to our palace, where we'll show

What's yet behind that's meet you all should
    know.

Measure for Measure (Act V, Scene i)

Daylight and champain discovers not more. This is open. I will be proud, I will read politic authors, I will baffle Sir Toby, I will wash off gross acquaintance, I will be point-devise the very man. I do not now fool myself to let imagination jade me; for every reason excites to this, that my lady loves me. She did commend my yellow stockings of late, she did praise my leg being cross-garter'd; and in this she manifests herself to my love, and with a kind of injunction drives me to these habits of her liking. I thank my stars I am happy. I will be strange, stout, in yellow stockings, and cross-garter'd, even with the swiftness of putting on. Jove and my stars be praised!

Twelfth Night; Or, What You Will (Act II, Scene v)

How like a winter hath my absence been
From thee, the pleasure of the fleeting year!
What freezings have I felt, what dark days seen!
What old December's bareness everywhere!
And yet this time removed was summer's time;
The teeming autumn, big with rich increase,
Bearing the wanton burden of the prime,
Like widow'd wombs after their lords' decease:
Yet this abundant issue seem'd to me
But hope of orphans, and unfather'd fruit;
For summer and his pleasures wait on thee,
And, thou away, the very birds are mute:
Or, if they sing, 'tis with so dull a cheer,
That leaves look pale, dreading the winter's
    near.

"Sonnet XCVII"

Poor soul, the centre of my sinful earth,
My sinful earth these rebel powers array,
Why dost thou pine within and suffer dearth,
Painting thy outward walls so costly gay?
Why so large cost, having so short a lease,
Dost thou upon thy fading mansion spend?
Shall worms, inheritors of this excess,
Eat up thy charge? Is this thy body's end?
Then soul, live thou upon thy servant's loss,
And let that pine to aggravate thy store;
Buy terms divine in selling hours of dross;
Within be fed, without be rich no more:
So shall thou feed on Death, that feeds on men,
And Death once dead, there's no more dying
   then.

"Sonnet CXLVI"

O Pandarus! I tell thee, Pandarus—
When I do tell thee there my hopes lie drown'd,
Reply not in how many fathoms deep
They lie indrench'd. I tell thee I am mad
In Cressid's love. Thou answer'st 'She is fair'—
Pourest in the open ulcer of my heart—
Her eyes, her hair, her cheek, her gait, her voice,
Handlest in thy discourse. O, that her hand,
In whose comparison all whites are ink
Writing their own reproach; to whose soft
  seizure
The cygnet's down is harsh, and spirit of sense
Hard as the palm of ploughman! This thou
  tell'st me,
As true thou tell'st me, when I say I love her;
But, saying thus, instead of oil and balm,
Thou lay'st in every gash that love hath given me
The knife that made it.

Troilus and Cressida (Act I, Scene i)

These flow'rs are like the pleasures of the
   world;
This bloody man, the care on't. I hope I dream;
For so I thought I was a cave-keeper,
And cook to honest creatures. But 'tis not so;
'Twas but a bolt of nothing, shot at nothing,
Which the brain makes of fumes. Our very eyes
Are sometimes, like our judgments, blind. Good
   faith,
I tremble still with fear; but if there be
Yet left in heaven as small a drop of pity
As a wren's eye, fear'd gods, a part of it!
The dream's here still. Even when I wake it is
Without me, as within me; not imagin'd, felt.
A headless man? The garments of Posthumus?
I know the shape of's leg; this is his hand,
His foot Mercurial, his Martial thigh,
The brawns of Hercules; but his Jovial face—
Murder in heaven! How! 'Tis gone. Pisanio . . .
Conspir'd with that irregulous devil, Cloten,
Hath here cut off my lord.

Cymbeline (Act IV, Scene ii)

As I do live by food, I met a fool,

Who laid him down and bask'd him in the sun,

And rail'd on Lady Fortune in good terms,

In good set terms—and yet a motley fool.

'Good morrow, fool,' quoth I; 'No, sir,' quoth he,

'Call me not fool till heaven hath sent me
    fortune.'

And then he drew a dial from his poke,

And, looking on it with lack-lustre eye,

Says very wisely, 'It is ten o'clock;

Thus we may see,' quoth he, 'how the world wags;

'Tis but an hour ago since it was nine;

And after one hour more 'twill be eleven;

And so, from hour to hour, we ripe and ripe,

And then, from hour to hour, we rot and rot;

And thereby hangs a tale.'

As You Like It (Act II, Scene vii)

Lo! in the orient when the gracious light
Lifts up his burning head, each under eye
Doth homage to his new-appearing sight,
Serving with looks his sacred majesty;
And having climb'd the steep-up heavenly hill,
Resembling strong youth in his middle age,
Yet mortal looks adore his beauty still,
Attending on his golden pilgrimage:
But when from highmost pitch, with weary car,
Like feeble age, he reeleth from the day,
The eyes, 'fore duteous, now converted are
From his low tract, and look another way:
So thou, thyself outgoing in thy noon:
Unlook'd, on diest unless thou get a son.

"Sonnet VII"

Against that time, if ever that time come,
When I shall see thee frown on my defects,
When as thy love hath cast his utmost sum,
Call'd to that audit by advis'd respects;
Against that time when thou shalt strangely
    pass,
And scarcely greet me with that sun, thine eye,
When love, converted from the thing it was,
Shall reasons find of settled gravity;
Against that time do I ensconce me here,
Within the knowledge of mine own desert,
And this my hand, against my self uprear,
To guard the lawful reasons on thy part:
To leave poor me thou hast the strength of laws,
Since why to love I can allege no cause.

"Sonnet XLIX"

CHAPTER SIX

A Classic Q & A

In this chapter, you'll have to answer the fun (and often ridiculous) questions we've provided. Finding an answer in the puzzle may be a little tricky, so feel free to use a little imagination and a lot of creativity to uncover the possibilities for responses. As you can see from our blackout example, your message may not 100 percent truthful when all is said and done, but it's guaranteed to be absolutely hilarious! Now, the real question is: Are you ready for this challenge?

How did it feel when you lost your favorite childhood pet?

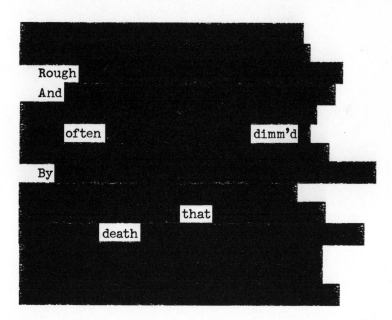

"Sonnet XVIII"

Message: Rough And often dimm'd By that death

Describe your best friend.

Love is too young to know what conscience is,
Yet who knows not conscience is born of love?
Then, gentle cheater, urge not my amiss,
Lest guilty of my faults thy sweet self prove:
For, thou betraying me, I do betray
My nobler part to my gross body's treason;
My soul doth tell my body that he may
Triumph in love; flesh stays no farther reason,
But rising at thy name doth point out thee,
As his triumphant prize. Proud of this pride,
He is contented thy poor drudge to be,
To stand in thy affairs, fall by thy side.
No want of conscience hold it that I call
Her 'love,' for whose dear love I rise and fall.

"Sonnet CLI"

What is the best trip you've ever been on?

Ye that on the sands with printless foot
Do chase the ebbing Neptune, and do fly him
When he comes back; you demi-puppets that
By moonshine do the green sour ringlets make,
Whereof the ewe not bites; and you whose
  pastime
Is to make midnight mushrooms, that rejoice
To hear the solemn curfew; by whose aid—
Weak masters though ye be—I have be-dimm'd
The noontide sun, call'd forth the mutinous
  winds,
And 'twixt the green sea and the azur'd vault
Set roaring war. To the dread rattling thunder
Have I given fire, and rifted Jove's stout oak
With his own bolt . . .
I'll break my staff,
Bury it certain fathoms in the earth,
And deeper than did ever plummet sound
I'll drown my book.

The Tempest (Act V, Scene i)

109

What are you afraid of?

O, I am out of breath in this fond chase!
The more my prayer, the lesser is my grace.
Happy is Hermia, wheresoe'er she lies,
For she hath blessed and attractive eyes.
How came her eyes so bright? Not with salt
  tears;
If so, my eyes are oft'ner wash'd than hers.
No, no, I am as ugly as a bear,
For beasts that meet me run away for fear;
Therefore no marvel though Demetrius
Do, as a monster, fly my presence thus.
What wicked and dissembling glass of mine
Made me compare with Hermia's sphery eyne?
But who is here? Lysander! on the ground!
Dead, or asleep? I see no blood, no wound.
Lysander, if you live, good sir, awake.

Midsummer-Night's Dream (Act II, Scene ii)

What is your favorite childhood memory?

Sweet love, renew thy force; be it not said
Thy edge should blunter be than appetite,
Which but to-day by feeding is allay'd,
To-morrow sharpened in his former might:
So, love, be thou, although to-day thou fill
Thy hungry eyes, even till they wink with
   fulness,
To-morrow see again, and do not kill
The spirit of love, with a perpetual dulness.
Let this sad interim like the ocean be
Which parts the shore, where two contracted new
Come daily to the banks, that when they see
Return of love, more blest may be the view;
Or call it winter, which being full of care,
Makes summer's welcome, thrice more wished,
   more rare.

"Sonnet LVI"

What did you dream about last night?

I have almost forgot the taste of fears:
The time has been, my senses would have cool'd
To hear a night-shriek, and my fell of hair
Would at a dismal treatise rouse and stir
As life were in't. I have supp'd full with
    horrors;
Direness, familiar to my slaughterous thoughts,
Cannot once start me . . .
She should have died hereafter;
There would have been a time for such a word.
Tomorrow, and tomorrow, and tomorrow
Creeps in this petty pace from day to day
To the last syllable of recorded time;
And all our yesterdays have lighted fools
The way to dusty death. Out, out, brief candle!
Life's but a walking shadow, a poor player
That struts and frets his hour upon the stage
And then is heard no more. It is a tale
Told by an idiot, full of sound and fury,
Signifying nothing.

Macbeth (Act V, Scene v)

What's the worst pick-up line you've heard?

Hum, I have heard
That guilty creatures, sitting at a play,
Have by the very cunning of the scene
Been struck so to the soul that presently
They have proclaim'd their malefactions;
For murther, though it have no tongue, will
  speak
With most miraculous organ, I'll have these
  Players
Play something like the murder of my father
Before mine uncle. I'll observe his looks;
I'll tent him to the quick. If he but blench,
I know my course. The spirit that I have seen
May be a devil; and the devil hath power
T' assume a pleasing shape; yea, and perhaps
Out of my weakness and my melancholy,
As he is very potent with such spirits,
Abuses me to damn me. I'll have grounds
More relative than this. The play's the thing
Wherein I'll catch the conscience of the King.

Hamlet, Prince of Denmark (Act II, Scene ii)

Describe your best birthday so far.

Not from the stars do I my judgement pluck;
And yet methinks I have astronomy,
But not to tell of good or evil luck,
Of plagues, of dearths, or seasons' quality;
Nor can I fortune to brief minutes tell,
Pointing to each his thunder, rain and wind,
Or say with princes if it shall go well
By oft predict that I in heaven find:
But from thine eyes my knowledge I derive,
And constant stars in them I read such art
As 'Truth and beauty shall together thrive,
If from thyself, to store thou wouldst convert';
Or else of thee this I prognosticate:
'Thy end is truth's and beauty's doom and date.'

"Sonnet XIV"

What is the best gift you've ever gotten?

O, reason not the need! Our basest beggars
Are in the poorest thing superfluous.
Allow not nature more than nature needs,
Man's life is cheap as beast's. Thou art a lady:
If only to go warm were gorgeous,
Why, nature needs not what thou gorgeous wear'st
Which scarcely keeps thee warm. But, for true
   need—
You heavens, give me that patience, patience I
   need!
You see me here, you gods, a poor old man,
As full of grief as age; wretched in both.
If it be you that stirs these daughters' hearts
Against their father, fool me not so much
To bear it tamely; touch me with noble anger,
And let not women's weapons, water drops,
Stain my man's cheeks!
. . . No, I'll not weep.
I have full cause of weeping, but this heart
Shall break into a hundred thousand flaws
Or ere I'll weep. O fool, I shall go mad!

King Lear (Act II, Scene iv)

CHAPTER SEVEN

A Little Faux Wisdom

What's the best part of getting Chinese takeout? The fortune cookie, of course! In this chapter, you'll try your hand at creating some of your very own, so get ready to summon your inner Confucius. You'll have to use the words in the following passages to form a profound statement worthy of a cookie. If you're having trouble coming up with some sage advice, look to our blackout example for guidance.

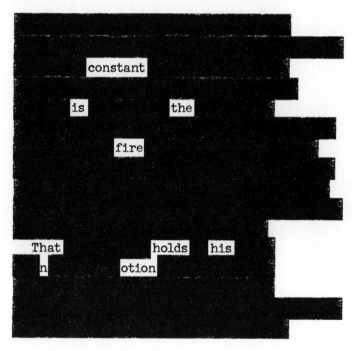

Julius Ceasar (Act III, Scene i)

Message: constant is the fire That holds his notion

123

You see me, Lord Bassanio, where I stand,
Such as I am . . .
Happy in this, she is not yet so old
But she may learn; happier than this,
She is not bred so dull but she can learn;
Happiest of all is that her gentle spirit
Commits itself to yours to be directed,
As from her lord, her governor, her king.
Myself and what is mine to you and yours
Is now converted. But now I was the lord
Of this fair mansion, master of my servants,
Queen o'er myself; and even now, but now,
This house, these servants, and this same
    myself,
Are yours—my lord's. I give them with this ring,
Which when you part from, lose, or give away,
Let it presage the ruin of your love,
And be my vantage to exclaim on you.

Merchant of Venice (Act III, Scene ii)

125

Thy glass will show thee how thy beauties wear,
Thy dial how thy precious minutes waste;
These vacant leaves thy mind's imprint will
  bear,
And of this book, this learning mayst thou taste.
The wrinkles which thy glass will truly show
Of mouthed graves will give thee memory;
Thou by thy dial's shady stealth mayst know
Time's thievish progress to eternity.
Look! what thy memory cannot contain,
Commit to these waste blanks, and thou shalt
  find
Those children nursed, deliver'd from thy brain,
To take a new acquaintance of thy mind.
These offices, so oft as thou wilt look,
Shall profit thee and much enrich thy book.

"Sonnet LXXVII"

Let me not to the marriage of true minds
Admit impediments. Love is not love
Which alters when it alteration finds,
Or bends with the remover to remove:
O, no! it is an ever-fixed mark,
That looks on tempests and is never shaken;
It is the star to every wandering bark,
Whose worth's unknown, although his height be
taken.
Love's not Time's fool, though rosy lips and
cheeks
Within his bending sickle's compass come;
Love alters not with his brief hours and weeks,
But bears it out even to the edge of doom.
If this be error and upon me prov'd,
I never writ, nor no man ever lov'd.

"Sonnet CXVI"

He that hath a beard is more than a youth, and he that hath no beard is less than a man; and he that is more than a youth is not for me; and he that is less than a man, I am not for him. Therefore I will even take sixpence in earnest of the berrord and lead his apes into hell . . . there will the devil meet me like an old cuckold with horns on his head, and say 'Get you to heaven, Beatrice, get you to heaven. Here's no place for you maids.' So deliver I up my apes, and away to Saint Peter—for the heavens. He shows me where the bachelors sit, and there live we as merry as the day is long.

Much Ado About Nothing (Act II, Scene i)

Farewell till then. I will go lose myself,
And wander up and down to view the city . . .
He that commends me to mine own content
Commends me to the thing I cannot get.
I to the world am like a drop of water
That in the ocean seeks another drop,
Who, falling there to find his fellow forth,
Unseen, inquisitive, confounds himself.
So I, to find a mother and a brother,
In quest of them, unhappy, lose myself.
Here comes the almanac of my true date.
What now? How chance thou art return'd so soon?
. . . . I am not in a sportive humour now;
Tell me, and dally not, where is the money?
We being strangers here, how dar'st thou trust
So great a charge from thine own custody?

Comedy of Errors (Act I, Scene ii)

Mine eye hath play'd the painter and hath
   stell'd,
Thy beauty's form in table of my heart;
My body is the frame wherein 'tis held,
And perspective it is best painter's art.
For through the painter must you see his skill,
To find where your true image pictur'd lies,
Which in my bosom's shop is hanging still,
That hath his windows glazed with thine eyes.
Now see what good turns eyes for eyes have done:
Mine eyes have drawn thy shape, and thine for me
Are windows to my breast, where-through the sun
Delights to peep, to gaze therein on thee;
Yet eyes this cunning want to grace their art,
They draw but what they see, know not the heart.

"Sonnet XXIV"

Two households, both alike in dignity,

In fair Verona, where we lay our scene,

From ancient grudge break to new mutiny,

Where civil blood makes civil hands unclean.

From forth the fatal loins of these two foes

A pair of star-cross'd lovers take their life;

Whose misadventur'd piteous overthrows

Doth with their death bury their parents' strife.

The fearful passage of their death-mark'd love,

And the continuance of their parents' rage,

Which, but their children's end, naught could
   remove,

Is now the two hours' traffic of our stage;

The which if you with patient ears attend,

What here shall miss, our toil shall strive to
   mend.

Romeo and Juliet (Prologue)

Hard to seem won; but I was won, my lord,
With the first glance that ever-pardon me.
If I confess much, you will play the tyrant.
I love you now; but till now not so much
But I might master it. In faith, I lie;
My thoughts were like unbridled children, grown
Too headstrong for their mother. See, we fools!
Why have I blabb'd? Who shall be true to us,
When we are so unsecret to ourselves?
But, though I lov'd you well, I woo'd you not;
And yet, good faith, I wish'd myself a man,
Or that we women had men's privilege
Of speaking first. Sweet, bid me hold my tongue,
For in this rapture I shall surely speak
The thing I shall repent. See, see, your silence,
Cunning in dumbness, from my weakness draws
My very soul of counsel. Stop my mouth.

Troilus and Cressida (Act III, Scene ii)

Weary with toil, I haste me to my bed,
The dear respose for limbs with travel tir'd;
But then begins a journey in my head
To work my mind, when body's work's expired:
For then my thoughts—from far where I abide—
Intend a zealous pilgrimage to thee,
And keep my drooping eyelids open wide,
Looking on darkness which the blind do see:
Save that my soul's imaginary sight
Presents thy shadow to my sightless view,
Which, like a jewel hung in ghastly night,
Makes black night beauteous, and her old face
    new.
Lo! thus, by day my limbs, by night my mind,
For thee, and for myself, no quiet find.

"Sonnet XXVII"

When my love swears that she is made of truth,
I do believe her though I know she lies,
That she might think me some untutor'd youth,
Unlearned in the world's false subtleties.
Thus vainly thinking that she thinks me young,
Although she knows my days are past the best,
Simply I credit her false-speaking tongue:
On both sides thus is simple truth suppressed:
But wherefore says she not she is unjust?
And wherefore say not I that I am old?
O! love's best habit is in seeming trust,
And age in love, loves not to have years told:
Therefore I lie with her, and she with me,
And in our faults by lies we flatter'd be.

"Sonnet CXXXVIII"

CHAPTER EIGHT

On the Contrary

You'll find out if opposites really attract in this challenging chapter. In order to solve the following puzzles, you'll have to create a contrasting message from the content we've provided. That means that if a passage revolves around the gruesome murder of a king, you'll have to undo the deed and quickly. Some puzzles will be harder than others, so if you get stumped, just make sure the theme of each message is completely different from the story as seen in the example we've given.

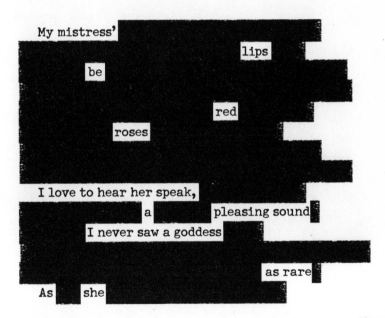

"Sonnet CXXX"

Message: My mistress' lips be red roses/I love to hear her speak, a pleasing sound/I never saw a goddess as rare as she

Full many a glorious morning have I seen
Flatter the mountain tops with sovereign eye,
Kissing with golden face the meadows green,
Gilding pale streams with heavenly alchemy;
Anon permit the basest clouds to ride
With ugly rack on his celestial face,
And from the forlorn world his visage hide,
Stealing unseen to west with this disgrace:
Even so my sun one early morn did shine,
With all triumphant splendour on my brow;
But out! alack! he was but one hour mine,
The region cloud hath mask'd him from me now.
Yet him for this my love no whit disdaineth;
Suns of the world may stain when heaven's sun
   staineth.

"Sonnet XXXIII"

What potions have I drunk of Siren tears,

Distill'd from limbecks foul as hell within,

Applying fears to hopes, and hopes to fears,

Still losing when I saw myself to win!

What wretched errors hath my heart committed,

Whilst it hath thought itself so blessed never!

How have mine eyes out of their spheres been
    fitted,

In the distraction of this madding fever!

O benefit of ill! now I find true

That better is, by evil still made better;

And ruin'd love, when it is built anew,

Grows fairer than at first, more strong, far
    greater.

So I return rebuk'd to my content,

And gain by ill thrice more than I have spent.

"Sonnet CXIX"

If by your art, my dearest father, you have
Put the wild waters in this roar, allay them.
The sky, it seems, would pour down stinking pitch,
But that the sea, mounting to th' welkin's cheek,
Dashes the fire out. O, I have suffered
With those that I saw suffer! A brave vessel,
Who had no doubt some noble creature in her,
Dash'd all to pieces! O, the cry did knock
Against my very heart! Poor souls, they perish'd.
Had I been any god of power, I would
Have sunk the sea within the earth or ere
It should the good ship so have swallow'd and
The fraughting souls within her.

The Tempest (Act I, Scene ii)

Howl, howl, howl, howl! O, you are men of stone.
Had I your tongues and eyes, I'll use them so
That heaven's vault should crack. She's gone for
ever!
I know when one is dead, and when one lives.
She's dead as earth. Lend me a looking glass.
If that her breath will mist or stain the stone,
Why, then she lives . . .
This feather stirs; she lives! If it be so,
It is a chance which does redeem all sorrows
That ever I have felt . . .
A plague upon you, murderers, traitors all!
I might have sav'd her; now she's gone for ever!
Cordelia, Cordelia! stay a little. Ha!
What is't thou say'st, Her voice was ever soft,
Gentle, and low—an excellent thing in woman.
I kill'd the slave that was a-hanging thee.

King Lear (Act V, Scene iii)

Those parts of thee that the world's eye doth
   view
Want nothing that the thought of hearts can
   mend;
All tongues—the voice of souls—give thee that
   due,
Uttering bare truth, even so as foes commend.
Thy outward thus with outward praise is
   crown'd;
But those same tongues, that give thee so thine
   own,
In other accents do this praise confound
By seeing farther than the eye hath shown.
They look into the beauty of thy mind,
And that in guess they measure by thy deeds;
Then—churls—their thoughts, although their
   eyes were kind,
To thy fair flower add the rank smell of weeds:
But why thy odour matcheth not thy show,
The soil is this, that thou dost common grow.

"Sonnet LXIX"

You, my lords,

Look on her, mark her well; be but about

To say 'She is a goodly lady' and

The justice of your hearts will thereto ad

''Tis pity she's not honest—honourable.'

Praise her but for this her without-door form,

Which on my faith deserves high speech, and
   straight

The shrug, the hum or ha, these petty brands

That calumny doth use—O, I am out!—

That mercy does, for calumny will sear

Virtue itself—these shrugs, these hum's and
   ha's,

When you have said she's goodly, come between,

Ere you can say she's honest. But be't known,

From him that has most cause to grieve it
   should be,

She's an adultress.

Winter's Tale (Act II, Scene i)

'Tis only title thou disdain'st in her, the which
I can build up. Strange is it that our bloods,
Of colour, weight, and heat, pour'd all together,
Would quite confound distinction, yet stand off
In differences so mighty. If she be
All that is virtuous—save what thou dislik'st,
A poor physician's daughter—thou dislik'st
Of virtue for the name; but do not so.
From lowest place when virtuous things proceed,
The place is dignified by the doer's deed;
Where great additions swell's, and virtue none,
It is a dropsied honour. Good alone
Is good without a name. Vileness is so:
The property by what it is should go,
Not by the title. She is young, wise, fair;
In these to nature she's immediate heir;
And these breed honour . . .
If thou canst like this creature as a maid,
I can create the rest. Virtue and she
Is her own dower; honour and wealth from me.

All's Well That Ends Well (Act II, Scene iii)

If I do prove her haggard,
Though that her jesses were my dear heartstrings,
I'd whistle her off and let her down the wind
To prey at fortune. Haply, for I am black
And have not those soft parts of conversation
That chamberers have, or for I am declined
Into the vale of years—yet that's not much—
She's gone. I am abused, and my relief
Must be to loathe her. O curse of marriage,
That we can call these delicate creatures ours,
And not their appetites! I had rather be a toad,
And live upon the vapor of a dungeon,
Than keep a corner in the thing I love
For others' uses. Yet, 'tis the plague of great
  ones:
Prerogatived are they less than the base;
'Tis destiny unshunnable, like death.
Even then this forked plague is fated to us
When we do quicken.

Othello, the Moor of Venice (Act III, Scene iii)

CHAPTER NINE

A Syllabic Musing

This chapter is sure to cause a rukus! To complete these lively puzzles, you'll have to create a message using two filler words and words with a certain number of syllables. Sure, you'll probably be able to handle one-syllabled words, but what about two- or three-syllabled words? You may find it helpful to reference the message we've created or sound out the words if you're having a hard time figuring out the number of syllables in each word.

Create a message using two-syllabled words.

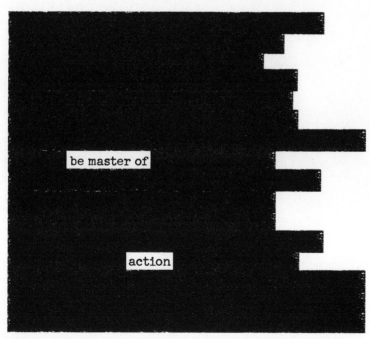

be master of

action

Taming of the Shrew (Act III, Scene ii)

Message: be master of action

163

Create a message using one-syllabled words.

I have had a most rare vision. I have had a dream, past the wit of man to say what dream it was. Man is but an ass if he go about to expound this dream. Methought I was—there is no man can tell what. Methought I was, and methought I had, but man is but a patch'd fool, if he will offer to say what methought I had. The eye of man hath not heard, the ear of man hath not seen, man's hand is not able to taste, his tongue to conceive, nor his heart to report, what my dream was. I will get Peter Quince to write a ballad of this dream. It shall be call'd 'Bottom's Dream,' because it hath no bottom; and I will sing it in the latter end of a play, before the Duke. Peradventure, to make it the more gracious, I shall sing it at her death.

Midsummer-Night's Dream (Act IV, Scene i)

Create a message using two-syllabled words.

Thy husband is thy lord, thy life, thy keeper,
Thy head, thy sovereign; one that cares for thee,
And for thy maintenance commits his body
To painful labour both by sea and land,
To watch the night in storms, the day in cold,
Whilst thou liest warm at home, secure and safe;
And craves no other tribute at thy hands
But love, fair looks, and true obedience—
Too little payment for so great a debt . . .
My mind hath been as big as one of yours,
My heart as great, my reason haply more,
To bandy word for word and frown for frown;
But now I see our lances are but straws,
Our strength as weak, our weakness past compare,
That seeming to be most which we indeed least
    are.
Then vail your stomachs, for it is no boot,
And place your hands below your husband's foot;
In token of which duty, if he please,
My hand is ready, may it do him ease.

Taming of the Shrew (Act V, Scene ii)

Create a message using two-syllabled words.

To me, fair friend, you never can be old,
For as you were when first your eye I ey'd,
Such seems your beauty still. Three winters cold,
Have from the forests shook three summers'
   pride,
Three beauteous springs to yellow autumn turn'd,
In process of the seasons have I seen,
Three April perfumes in three hot Junes burn'd,
Since first I saw you fresh, which yet are green.
Ah! yet doth beauty like a dial-hand,
Steal from his figure, and no pace perceiv'd;
So your sweet hue, which methinks still doth
   stand,
Hath motion, and mine eye may be deceiv'd:
For fear of which, hear this thou age unbred:
Ere you were born was beauty's summer dead.

"Sonnet CIV"

Create a message using one-syllabled words.

This she? No; this is Diomed's Cressida.
If beauty have a soul, this is not she;
If souls guide vows, if vows be sanctimonies,
If sanctimony be the god's delight,
If there be rule in unity itself,
This was not she. O madness of discourse,
That cause sets up with and against itself!
Bifold authority! where reason can revolt
Without perdition, and loss assume all reason
Without revolt: this is, and is not, Cressid.
Within my soul there doth conduce a fight
Of this strange nature, that a thing inseparate
Divides more wider than the sky and earth;
And yet the spacious breadth of this division
Admits no orifex for a point as subtle
As Ariachne's broken woof to enter.
Instance, O instance! strong as Pluto's gates:
Cressid is mine, tied with the bonds of heaven.
Instance, O instance! strong as heaven itself:
The bonds of heaven are slipp'd, dissolv'd, and
   loos'd.

Troilus and Cressida (Act V, Scene ii)

Create a message using one-syllabled words.

Now, out of doubt, Antipholus is mad,
Else would he never so demean himself.
A ring he hath of mine worth forty ducats,
And for the same he promis'd me a chain;
Both one and other he denies me now.
The reason that I gather he is mad,
Besides this present instance of his rage,
Is a mad tale he told to-day at dinner
Of his own doors being shut against his
   entrance.
Belike his wife, acquainted with his fits,
On purpose shut the doors against his way.
My way is now to hie home to his house,
And tell his wife that, being lunatic,
He rush'd into my house and took perforce
My ring away. This course I fittest choose,
For forty ducats is too much to lose.

Comedy of Errors (Act IV, Scene iii)

Create a message using two-syllabled words.

I would have broke mine eyestrings, crack'd them
  but
To look upon him, till the diminution
Of space had pointed him sharp as my needle;
Nay, followed him till he had melted from
The smallness of a gnat to air, and then
Have turn'd mine eye and wept. But, good Pisanio,
When shall we hear from him?
... I did not take my leave of him, but had
Most pretty things to say. Ere I could tell him
How I would think on him at certain hours
Such thoughts and such; or I could make him swear
The shes of Italy should not betray
Mine interest and his honour; or have charg'd him,
At the sixth hour of morn, at noon, at midnight,
T' encounter me with orisons, for then
I am in heaven for him; or ere I could
Give him that parting kiss which I had set
Betwixt two charming words, comes in my father,
And like the tyrannous breathing of the north
Shakes all our buds from growing.

Cymbeline (Act I, Scene iii)

Create a message using one-syllabled words.

O! never say that I was false of heart,
Though absence seem'd my flame to qualify,
As easy might I from my self depart
As from my soul which in thy breast doth lie:
That is my home of love: if I have rang'd,
Like him that travels, I return again;
Just to the time, not with the time exchang'd,
So that myself bring water for my stain.
Never believe though in my nature reign'd,
All frailties that besiege all kinds of blood,
That it could so preposterously be stain'd,
To leave for nothing all thy sum of good;
For nothing this wide universe I call,
Save thou, my rose, in it thou art my all.

"Sonnet CIX"

Create a message using two-syllabled words.

When forty winters shall besiege thy brow,
And dig deep trenches in thy beauty's field,
Thy youth's proud livery so gazed on now,
Will be a tatter'd weed of small worth held:
Then being asked, where all thy beauty lies,
Where all the treasure of thy lusty days;
To say, within thine own deep sunken eyes,
Were an all-eating shame, and thriftless praise.
How much more praise deserv'd thy beauty's use,
If thou couldst answer 'This fair child of mine
Shall sum my count, and make my old excuse,'
Proving his beauty by succession thine!
This were to be new made when thou art old,
And see thy blood warm when thou feel'st it cold.

"Sonnet II"

CHAPTER TEN

One for the Books

The challenge in this chapter isn't in creating a message, but picking the *right* words. You can only use one word per line to complete each puzzle, and don't even think about cheating on this one—you can only use ink! If you're having trouble though, remember that you don't have to use every single line to complete your message.

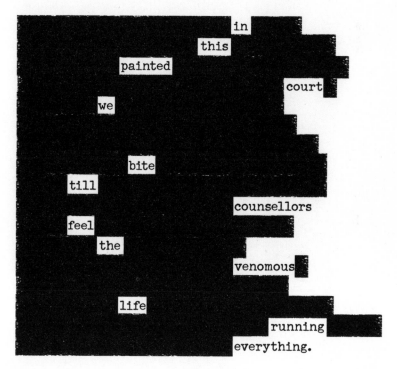

As You Like It (Act II, Scene i)

Message: in this painted court we bite till counsellors feel the venomous life running everything.

O, pardon me, thou bleeding piece of earth,
That I am meek and gentle with these butchers!
Thou art the ruins of the noblest man
That ever lived in the tide of times.
Woe to the hand that shed this costly blood!
Over thy wounds now do I prophesy
(Which like dumb mouths do ope their ruby lips
To beg the voice and utterance of my tongue)
A curse shall light upon the limbs of men;
Domestic fury and fierce civil strife
Shall cumber all the parts of Italy;
Blood and destruction shall be so in use,
And dreadful objects so familiar,
That mothers shall but smile when they behold
Their infants quarter'd with the hands of war;
All pity choked with custom of fell deeds,
And Caesar's spirit ranging for revenge,
With Ate by his side come hot from hell,
Shall in these confines with a monarch's voice
Cry "Havoc!" and let slip the dogs of war,
That this foul deed shall smell above the earth
With carrion men, groaning for burial.

Julius Ceasar (Act III, Scene i)

That thou hast her it is not all my grief,
And yet it may be said I loved her dearly;
That she hath thee is of my wailing chief,
A loss in love that touches me more nearly.
Loving offenders thus I will excuse ye:
Thou dost love her, because thou know'st I
   love her;
And for my sake even so doth she abuse me,
Suffering my friend for my sake to approve her.
If I lose thee, my loss is my love's gain,
And losing her, my friend hath found that loss;
Both find each other, and I lose both twain,
And both for my sake lay on me this cross:
But here's the joy; my friend and I are one;
Sweet flattery! then she loves but me alone.

"Sonnet XLII"

Upon her landing, Antony sent to her,
Invited her to supper. She replied
It should be better he became her guest;
Which she entreated. Our courteous Antony,
Whom ne'er the word of 'No' woman heard speak,
Being barber'd ten times o'er, goes to the feast,
And for his ordinary pays his heart
For what his eyes eat only . . .
I saw her once
Hop forty paces through the public street;
And, having lost her breath, she spoke, and
   panted,
That she did make defect perfection,
And, breathless, pow'r breathe forth . . .
Age cannot wither her, nor custom stale
Her infinite variety. Other women cloy
The appetites they feed, but she makes hungry
Where most she satisfies; for vilest things
Become themselves in her, that the holy priests
Bless her when she is riggish.

Antony and Cleopatra (Act II, Scene ii)

O! never say that I was false of heart,
Though absence seem'd my flame to qualify,
As easy might I from my self depart
As from my soul which in thy breast doth lie:
That is my home of love: if I have rang'd,
Like him that travels, I return again;
Just to the time, not with the time exchang'd,
So that myself bring water for my stain.
Never believe though in my nature reign'd,
All frailties that besiege all kinds of blood,
That it could so preposterously be stain'd,
To leave for nothing all thy sum of good;
For nothing this wide universe I call,
Save thou, my rose, in it thou art my all.

"Sonnet CIX"

Look on this letter, madam; here's my passport.

(Reads) 'When thou canst get the ring upon my
   finger, which never shall come off, and show
   me a child begotten of thy body that I am
   father to, then call me husband; but in such a
   "then" I write a "never."

This is a dreadful sentence . . .

Nothing in France until he has no wife!

Thou shalt have none, Rousillon, none in France

Then hast thou all again.

. . . And though I kill him not, I am the cause

His death was so effected.

. . . No; come thou home, Rousillon,

Whence honour but of danger wins a scar,

As oft it loses all. I will be gone.

My being here it is that holds thee hence.

Shall I stay here to do't? No, no, although

The air of paradise did fan the house,

And angels offic'd all. I will be gone.

All's Well That Ends Well (Act III, Scene ii)

When that I was and a little tiny boy,
With hey, ho, the wind and the rain,
A foolish thing was but a toy,
For the rain it raineth every day.
But when I came to man's estate,
With hey, ho, the wind and the rain,
'Gainst knaves and thieves men shut their gate,
For the rain it raineth every day.
But when I came, alas! to wive,
With hey, ho, the wind and the rain,
By swaggering could I never thrive,
For the rain it raineth every day.
But when I came unto my beds,
With hey, ho, the wind and the rain,
With toss-pots still had drunken heads,
For the rain it raineth every day.
A great while ago the world begun,
With hey, ho, the wind and the rain,
But that's all one, our play is done,
And we'll strive to please you every day.

Twelfth Night; Or, What You Will (Act V, Scene i)

'Tis one thing to be tempted, Escalus,
Another thing to fall. I not deny
The jury, passing on the prisoner's life,
May in the sworn twelve have a thief or two
Guiltier than him they try. What's open made
  to justice,
That justice seizes. What knows the laws
That thieves do pass on thieves? 'Tis very
  pregnant,
The jewel that we find, we stoop and take't,
Because we see it; but what we do not see
We tread upon, and never think of it.
You may not so extenuate his offence
For I have had such faults; but rather tell me,
When I, that censure him, do so offend,
Let mine own judgment pattern out my death,
And nothing come in partial.

Measure for Measure (Act II, Scene i)

With anger, with sickness, or with hunger, my lord; not with love. Prove that ever I lose more blood with love than I will get again with drinking, pick out mine eyes with a ballad-maker's pen and hang me up at the door of a brothel house for the sign of blind Cupid . . . If I do (fall), hang me in a bottle like a cat and shoot at me; and he that hits me, let him be clapp'd on the shoulder and call'd Adam . . . if ever the sensible Benedick bear it, pluck off the bull's horns and set them in my forehead, and let me be vilely painted, and in such great letters as they write 'Here is good horse to hire,' let them signify under my sign 'Here you may see Benedick the married man.'

Much Ado About Nothing (Act I, Scene i)

Like as the waves make towards the pebbled shore,
So do our minutes hasten to their end;
Each changing place with that which goes before,
In sequent toil all forwards do contend.
Nativity, once in the main of light,
Crawls to maturity, wherewith being crown'd,
Crooked eclipses 'gainst his glory fight,
And Time that gave doth now his gift confound.
Time doth transfix the flourish set on youth
And delves the parallels in beauty's brow,
Feeds on the rarities of nature's truth,
And nothing stands but for his scythe to mow:
And yet to times in hope, my verse shall stand.
Praising thy worth, despite his cruel hand.

"Sonnet LX"

CHAPTER ELEVEN

Alternating Tidings

Like the previous chapter, you'll have to find the perfect words to complete these puzzles, but this time we made sure to kick it up a notch. Unlike before, you'll only be able to use one word from every other line to create a message, which means you'll have to pay extra attention to what you black out. While choosing words line by line is definitely much more exciting, feel free to plan ahead if you can't figure out which ones you want to get rid of.

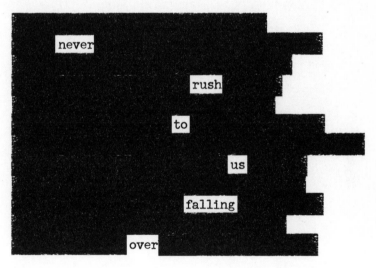

Midsummer-Night's Dream (Act II, Scene i)

Message: never rush to us falling over

Those lips that Love's own hand did make,
Breathed forth the sound that said 'I hate',
To me that languish'd for her sake:
But when she saw my woeful state,
Straight in her heart did mercy come,
Chiding that tongue that ever sweet
Was us'd in giving gentle doom;
And taught it thus anew to greet;
'I hate' she alter'd with an end,
That followed it as gentle day,
Doth follow night, who like a fiend
From heaven to hell is flown away.
'I hate', from hate away she threw,
And sav'd my life, saying 'not you'.

"Sonnet CXLV"

Why didst thou promise such a beauteous day,
And make me travel forth without my cloak,
To let base clouds o'ertake me in my way,
Hiding thy bravery in their rotten smoke?
'Tis not enough that through the cloud thou
    break,
To dry the rain on my storm-beaten face,
For no man well of such a salve can speak,
That heals the wound, and cures not the disgrace:
Nor can thy shame give physic to my grief;
Though thou repent, yet I have still the loss:
The offender's sorrow lends but weak relief
To him that bears the strong offence's cross.
Ah! but those tears are pearl which thy love
    sheds,
And they are rich and ransom all ill deeds.

"Sonnet XXXIV"

What if my house be troubled with a rat,
And I be pleas'd to give ten thousand ducats
To have it ban'd? What, are you answer'd yet?
Some men there are love not a gaping pig;
Some that are mad if they behold a cat;
And others, when the bagpipe sings i' th' nose,
Cannot contain their urine; for affection,
Mistress of passion, sways it to the mood
Of what it likes or loathes . . .
So can I give no reason, nor I will not,
More than a lodg'd hate and a certain loathing
I bear Antonio, that I follow thus
A losing suit against him. Are you answered?

Merchant of Venice (Act IV, Scene i)

My glass shall not persuade me I am old,
So long as youth and thou are of one date;
But when in thee time's furrows I behold,
Then look I death my days should expiate.
For all that beauty that doth cover thee,
Is but the seemly raiment of my heart,
Which in thy breast doth live, as thine in me:
How can I then be elder than thou art?
O! therefore love, be of thyself so wary
As I, not for myself, but for thee will;
Bearing thy heart, which I will keep so chary
As tender nurse her babe from faring ill.
Presume not on thy heart when mine is slain,
Thou gav'st me thine not to give back again.

"Sonnet XXII"

I do not know
One of my sex; no woman's face remember,
Save, from my glass, mine own; nor have I seen
More that I may call men than you, good friend,
And my dear father. How features are abroad,
I am skilless of; but, by my modesty,
The jewel in my dower, I would not wish
Any companion in the world but you;
Nor can imagination form a shape,
Besides yourself, to like of.
. . . dare not offer
What I desire to give, and much less take
What I shall die to want. But this is trifling;
And all the more it seeks to hide itself,
The bigger bulk it shows. Hence, bashful cunning!
And prompt me, plain and holy innocence!
I am your wife, if you will marry me;
If not, I'll die your maid. To be your fellow
You may deny me; but I'll be your servant,
Whether you will or no.

The Tempest (Act III, Scene i)

Others there are

Who, trimm'd in forms and visages of duty,

Keep yet their hearts attending on themselves,

And throwing but shows of service on their lords

Do well thrive by them; and when they have
  lined their coats

Do themselves homage. These fellows have some
  soul,

And such a one do I profess myself.

For, sir,

It is as sure as you are Roderigo,

Were I the Moor, I would not be Iago.

In following him, I follow but myself;

Heaven is my judge, not I for love and duty,

But seeming so, for my peculiar end.

For when my outward action doth demonstrate

The native act and figure of my heart

In complement extern, 'tis not long after

But I will wear my heart upon my sleeve

For daws to peck at: I am not what I am.

Othello, the Moor of Venice (Act I, Scene i)

The expense of spirit in a waste of shame
Is lust in action: and till action, lust
Is perjur'd, murderous, bloody, full of blame,
Savage, extreme, rude, cruel, not to trust;
Enjoy'd no sooner but despised straight;
Past reason hunted; and no sooner had,
Past reason hated, as a swallow'd bait,
On purpose laid to make the taker mad:
Mad in pursuit and in possession so;
Had, having, and in quest, to have extreme;
A bliss in proof,—and prov'd, a very woe;
Before, a joy propos'd; behind a dream.
All this the world well knows; yet none knows
  well
To shun the heaven that leads men to this hell.

"Sonnet CXXIX"

Too hot, too hot!
To mingle friendship far is mingling bloods.
I have tremor cordis on me; my heart dances,
But not for joy, not joy. This entertainment
May a free face put on; derive a liberty
From heartiness, from bounty, fertile bosom,
And well become the agent. 'T may, I grant;
But to be paddling palms and pinching fingers,
As now they are, and making practis'd smiles
As in a looking-glass; and then to sigh, as 'twere
The mort o' th' deer. O, that is entertainment
My bosom likes not, nor my brows! Mamillius,
Art thou my boy?

Winter's Tale (Act I, Scene ii)

Since I left you, mine eye is in my mind;
And that which governs me to go about
Doth part his function and is partly blind,
Seems seeing, but effectually is out;
For it no form delivers to the heart
Of bird, of flower, or shape which it doth latch:
Of his quick objects hath the mind no part,
Nor his own vision holds what it doth catch;
For if it see the rud'st or gentlest sight,
The most sweet favour or deformed'st creature,
The mountain or the sea, the day or night:
The crow, or dove, it shapes them to your feature.
Incapable of more, replete with you,
My most true mind thus maketh mine untrue.

"Sonnet CXIII"

Why came I hither but to that intent?

Think you a little din can daunt mine ears?

Have I not in my time heard lions roar?

Have I not heard the sea, puff'd up with winds,

Rage like an angry boar chafed with sweat?

Have I not heard great ordnance in the field,

And heaven's artillery thunder in the skies?

Have I not in a pitched battle heard

Loud 'larums, neighing steeds, and trumpets'
  clang?

And do you tell me of a woman's tongue,

That gives not half so great a blow to hear

As will a chestnut in a fariner's fire?

Tush! tush! fear boys with bugs.

Taming of the Shrew (Act I, Scene ii)

CHAPTER TWELVE

More than Symbols

By now you may feel like you've mastered these addicting puzzles, but you haven't seen anything yet! In this final chapter, you'll need to not only create a message, but also construct it in the shape of an object. Sure, our blackout sample may make this chapter look like a piece of cake, but once you get started, you'll definitely see that this challenge is easier said than done. Just remember that you don't have to stick to a certain area of the page, anywhere and any size will do as long as you develop your message in shape. Once you've finished, you'll have a blackout masterpiece truly worth showing of, so make sure you pass it along to friends!

Create a message in the shape of a rectangle.

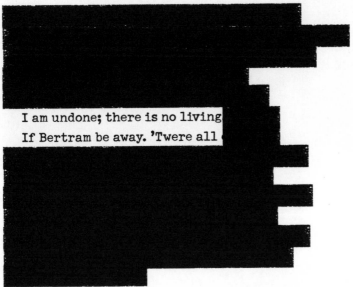

All's Well That Ends Well (Act I, Scene i)

Message: I am undone; there is no living If Bertram be away. 'Twere all

Create a message in the shape of a diamond.

The raven himself is hoarse
That croaks the fatal entrance of Duncan
Under my battlements. Come, you spirits
That tend on mortal thoughts, unsex me here
And fill me from the crown to the toe top-full
Of direst cruelty! Make thick my blood,
Stop up the access and passage to remorse,
That no compunctious visitings of nature
Shake my fell purpose nor keep peace between
The effect and it! Come to my woman's breasts,
And take my milk for gall, your murthering
    ministers,
Wherever in your sightless substances
You wait on nature's mischief! Come, thick night,
And pall thee in the dunnest smoke of hell
That my keen knife see not the wound it makes
Nor heaven peep through the blanket of the dark
To cry, "Hold, hold!"

Macbeth (Act I, Scene v)

Create a message in the shape of a square.

Dost thou not suspect my place? Dost thou not suspect my years? O that he were here to write me down an ass! But, masters, remember that I am an ass. Though it be not written down, yet forget not that I am an ass. No, thou villain, thou art full of piety, as shall be prov'd upon thee by good witness. I am a wise fellow; and which is more, an officer; and which is more, a householder; and which is more, as pretty a piece of flesh as any is in Messina, and one that knows the law, go to! and a rich fellow enough, go to! and a fellow that hath had losses; and one that hath two gowns and everything handsome about him. Bring him away. O that I had been writ down an ass!

Much Ado About Nothing (Act IV, Scene ii)

Create a message in the shape of a circle.

I have of late—but wherefore I know not—lost all my mirth, forgone all custom of exercises; and indeed, it goes so heavily with my disposition that this goodly frame, the earth, seems to me a sterile promontory; this most excellent canopy, the air, look you, this brave o'erhanging firmament, this majestical roof fretted with golden fire—why, it appeareth no other thing to me than a foul and pestilent congregation of vapours. What a piece of work is a man! how noble in reason! how infinite in faculties! in form and moving how express and admirable! in action how like an angel! in apprehension how like a god! the beauty of the world, the paragon of animals! And yet to me what is this quintessence of dust?

Hamlet, Prince of Denmark (Act II, Scene ii)

Create a message in the shape of a heart.

O Romeo, Romeo! wherefore art thou Romeo?
Deny thy father and refuse thy name;
Or, if thou wilt not, be but sworn my love,
And I'll no longer be a Capulet . . .
'Tis but thy name that is my enemy;
Thou art thyself, though not a Montague.
What's Montague? It is nor hand, nor foot,
Nor arm, nor face, nor any other part
Belonging to a man. O, be some other name!
What's in a name? That which we call a rose
By any other word would smell as sweet;
So Romeo would, were he not Romeo call'd,
Retain that dear perfection which he owes
Without that title. Romeo, doff thy name.
And for thy name which is no part of thee
Take all myself.

Romeo and Juliet (Act II, Scene i)

Create a message in the shape of a diamond.

From you have I been absent in the spring,
When proud-pied April, dress'd in all his trim,
Hath put a spirit of youth in every thing,
That heavy Saturn laugh'd and leap'd with him.
Yet nor the lays of birds, nor the sweet smell
Of different flowers in odour and in hue,
Could make me any summer's story tell,
Or from their proud lap pluck them where they
    grew:
Nor did I wonder at the lily's white,
Nor praise the deep vermilion in the rose;
They were but sweet, but figures of delight,
Drawn after you, you pattern of all those.
Yet seem'd it winter still, and you away,
As with your shadow I with these did play.

"Sonnet XCVIII"

Create a message in the shape of a rectangle.

Then hate me when thou wilt; if ever, now;
Now, while the world is bent my deeds to cross,
Join with the spite of fortune, make me bow,
And do not drop in for an after-loss:
Ah! do not, when my heart hath 'scap'd this
   sorrow,
Come in the rearward of a conquer'd woe;
Give not a windy night a rainy morrow,
To linger out a purpos'd overthrow.
If thou wilt leave me, do not leave me last,
When other petty griefs have done their spite,
But in the onset come: so shall I taste
At first the very worst of fortune's might;
And other strains of woe, which now seem woe,
Compar'd with loss of thee, will not seem so.

"Sonnet XC"

Create a message in the shape of a triangle.

I am not furnish'd like a beggar; therefore to beg will not become me. My way is to conjure you; and I'll begin with the women. I charge you, O women, for the love you bear to men, to like as much of this play as please you; and I charge you, O men, for the love you bear to women- as I perceive by your simp'ring none of you hates them- that between you and the women the play may please. If I were a woman, I would kiss as many of you as had beards that pleas'd me, complexions that lik'd me, and breaths that I defied not; and, I am sure, as many as have good beards, or good faces, or sweet breaths, will, for my kind offer, when I make curtsy, bid me farewell.

As You Like It (Epilogue)

Bibliography

Shakespeare, William. "All's Well That Ends Well." *Complete Works of Shakespeare*. Philadelphia: David McKay, 1887.

Shakespeare, William. "As You Like It." *Complete Works of Shakespeare*. Philadelphia: David McKay, 1887.

Shakespeare, William. "Comedy of Errors." *Complete Works of Shakespeare*. Philadelphia: David McKay, 1887.

Shakespeare, William. "Hamlet, Prince of Denmark." *Complete Works of Shakespeare*. Philadelphia: David McKay, 1887.

Shakespeare, William. "Julius Ceasar." *Complete Works of Shakespeare*. Philadelphia: David McKay, 1887.

Shakespeare, William. "Macbeth." *Complete Works of Shakespeare*. Philadelphia: David McKay, 1887.

Shakespeare, William. "Measure for Measure." *Complete Works of Shakespeare*. Philadelphia: David McKay, 1887.

Shakespeare, William. "Merchant of Venice." *Complete Works of Shakespeare*. Philadelphia: David McKay, 1887.

Shakespeare, William. "Midsummer-Night's Dream." *Complete Works of Shakespeare*. Philadelphia: David McKay, 1887.

Shakespeare, William. "Much Ado About Nothing." *Complete Works of Shakespeare*. Philadelphia: David McKay, 1887.

Shakespeare, William. "Othello, the Moor of Venice." *Complete Works of Shakespeare*. Philadelphia: David McKay, 1887.

Shakespeare, William. "Taming of the Shrew." *Complete Works of Shakespeare*. Philadelphia: David McKay, 1887.

Shakespeare, William. "The Tempest." *Complete Works of Shakespeare*. Philadelphia: David McKay, 1887.

Shakespeare, William. "Twelfth Night; Or, What You Will." *Complete Works of Shakespeare*. Philadelphia: David McKay, 1887.

Shakespeare, William. "Troilus and Cressida." *Complete Works of Shakespeare*. Philadelphia: David McKay, 1887.

Shakespeare, William. "Winter's Tale." *Complete Works of Shakespeare*. Philadelphia: David McKay, 1887.

Shakespeare, William. *Shakespeare's Sonnets*. Boston: Ticknor and Fields, 1865.